ANTICIPATING THE UNEXPECTED
Living a Blessed Life

By Leigh Ann Coats

Anticipating the Unexpected: Living a Blessed Life
Copyright © 2019 by Leigh Ann Coats

All rights reserved. No part of this book may be reproduced in any form, stored in a retrieval system or transmitted in any form by any means—electronic, mechanical, photocopy, recording, or otherwise—without the prior written permission of the author/publisher.

Unless otherwise indicated, Scriptures are taken from the *New American Standard Bible*, copyright © 1960, 1962, 1963, 1968, 1971, 1972, 1973, 1975, 1977 by The Lockman Foundation. Thomas Nelson Publishers.

Published by Sir Brody Books | Cleveland, Tennessee USA | sirbrody.com | @sirbrodybooks

ISBN 978-1-951551-00-1

Printed in the United States of America

Cover Design by Jennifer Griffin

Author Photo by KB Photography

To my children, David and Rachel.
You are special gifts from God and greatly loved.
What a rich spiritual heritage
you have been blessed with.
May you follow Jesus Christ
every day and bring glory to His Name.
Tell your children and grandchildren about the
awesome power of our God!

From the fullness of his grace we have all received one blessing after another. —John 1:16 (NIV)

CONTENTS

Foreword by Rod Bakker

1. A Blessed Life
    Jesus Christ is the ultimate channel of God's blessing.
2. Our Spiritual Heritage
    Our heritage is a channel of God's blessing.
3. Experiencing Angels
    Ministering angels are a channel of God's blessing.
4. His Grace Is Sufficient for Me
    Obstacles are a channel of God's blessing.
5. A Love Story
    Love is a channel of God's blessing.
6. Will You Meet Me in My Dreams?
    Dreams are a channel of God's blessing.
7. The Unseen Hands
    The supernatural is a channel of God's blessing.
8. I Am Not My Own
    Surrender is a channel of God's blessing.
9. Awareness of the Holy Spirit
    The Holy Spirit is a channel of God's blessing.

10. The Fingerprints of God
    Nature is a channel of God's blessing.
11. The Easter Egg
    Miracles are a channel of God's blessing.
12. Lessons in Suffering
    Suffering is a channel of God's blessing.
13. The Blessing of a Gift
    Gifts are a channel of God's blessing.
14. Kindred Spirits
    The community of believers, the church, is a channel of God's blessing.
15. "You Want Me to Do What?"
    Change is a channel of God's blessing.
16. "Help Me, Lord, I Am Sick of Myself!"
    Humility is a channel of God's blessing.
17. Which One Will It Be?
    You are a channel of God's blessing.

Appendix A: Easter Story Cookies
Appendix B: We Belong to God—We Are Not Our Own
Acknowledgments
Notes

FOREWORD

Shawn and Amanda were the perfect couple. Both people of deep Christian faith, Shawn and Amanda met while in college, fell in love, and were married. In the early years, Shawn worked in various ministries and played bass in a Christian band while Amanda was a director at Alternatives Pregnancy Center in Denver, Colorado, a life-affirming ministry to women with unplanned pregnancies. In time God blessed Shawn and Amanda with two beautiful children—a girl and a boy. After a few years of marriage, they moved to California, where Shawn began a construction management company. They settled into their new home and set about to live the life of which they had dreamed.

When Shawn and Amanda found there was another blessing on the way, they organized the nursery and readied themselves for this new addition. They were excited to find out they were expecting a little girl. However, they could never have prepared themselves for what was about to unfold in the next chapter of their lives.

Up to the moment of Tatum's birth, everyone anticipated another healthy baby to add to their growing family. What transpired was something different than the expected. Tatum was born with spina bifida—a neural tube defect of the spinal cord that can leave the infant child paralyzed, malformed, and fighting for life.

Tatum was rushed to The University of San Francisco Medical Center (USFMC), where she underwent a series of life-saving surgeries. For three weeks, the USFMC neonatal ICU was Tatum's home. Shawn and Amanda struggled to be at Tatum's bedside and attempt to keep home life semi-normal for their other two children, while working to keep their new company afloat.

During those difficult days, there was a multitude of calls for prayer across the country. People who never met Shawn or Amanda prayed for Tatum and her family. Amanda began a daily e-journal to keep friends and family informed of Tatum's progress. These journal entries, some of the most beautiful words I've read, provided a balm for Amanda's hurting heart.

Through Amanda's poignant and soul-searching words, many witnessed the pain, questions, faith, and grace of a mother's heart. Some days her words were filled with sorrow. Some days her words were filled with hope. Some days there was frustration and anger. But through all the ups and downs of those first weeks and months, there was the beautiful thread of a mother and father who trusted in God's goodness and the faithfulness of Jesus Christ.

Shawn and Amanda held on to one another. Together, they put their arms around Tatum and put their hope in the God who they knew would not let them go.

My wife and I visited Shawn and Amanda to meet baby Tatum when she was one year old. So many prayers had been prayed, and while there were reports that gave us reason to be hopeful that one day Tatum might gain use of her legs, we didn't know what to expect.

We were greeted in the front yard of a beautiful little home by my great niece and great nephew. There was excitement at our visit from Illinois. My fear abated just a bit, but I wasn't prepared for what came next.

We were ushered into the living room. There, in a standing device for paralyzed children, was a beautiful, smiling child who greeted us with arms spread wide, a huge smile, and a robust, "Hi!" Standing there was a loved and happy child if I'd ever seen one. It was evident that God answered the multitude of prayers for Tatum and her family. In the midst of daily challenges, it was clear that God's hand of blessing was over this happy little family.

Why are Shawn and Amanda happy? Because they are blessed! To many people, their joy might seem a contradiction, but here is a family who understands that because the Lord has them firmly in His grip, they have all they need. Like the Apostle Paul, Shawn and Amanda have learned the secret of being content with much or little, and perhaps most importantly, they have learned that God's grace is all they need.

My friend Leigh Ann Coats has learned many of the same lessons, and she writes about them in this book, *Anticipating the Unexpected*. There are times when being blessed is clearly a blessing and other times when being blessed comes with a burden we don't want to bear. Nonetheless, as people of faith, we know that we are blessed regardless of our circumstances, because we belong to God in Christ.

Jesus talked about blessed ones in the Sermon on the Mount. He began with eight short sayings, which at first glance make no sense. They tell us that people who are poor, mourning, and persecuted are blessed. But as with other apparent contradictions in the teaching of Jesus, the Beatitudes are filled with profound spiritual truth. When we look carefully at these eight verses in Matthew 5, we find these eight simple sayings of Jesus are a beautiful, multifaceted jewel that reveals the benefits of being chosen and blessed by God.

Jesus said that His disciples are happy. Of course, this means far more than merely feeling happy. It means, like Shawn and Amanda, there may be times that we don't feel happy at all, but we're still profoundly aware that we are blessed. We're blessed by the knowledge that no matter what life may throw at us, we still have the assurance that we are in God's hands, and in the end, we will receive in full the blessings that we only glimpse in this life.

I recommend this book to those whom, like Leigh Ann, have found that being blessed by the Lord can sometimes be a hard road to travel and at other times, unspeakable joy. You will find much in the pages of this book to bring peace to your soul, regardless of the lessons God is teaching you in your particular season of life.

Rev. Rodney J. Bakker
Faith Presbyterian Church, Retired
Quincy, Illinois

ANTICIPATING THE UNEXPECTED
Living a Blessed Life

By Leigh Ann Coats

CHAPTER 1
A BLESSED LIFE

Sitting in a restaurant, I overheard a woman say how blessed she was to experience good health. Another time, while shopping for groceries, the couple nearby was talking about how blessed they were to buy a new car. Conversations with parents at my children's school revealed the blessings of dream homes.

You hear it all the time: "I just received a raise," "We found the perfect parking space," "My daughter got an A on her paper," "Everything is going my way"—"*I am so blessed.*" It is common to hear people remark on their good fortune when they have health, wealth, and prosperity. Somewhere along the way, many come to believe that God wants us to be happy, healthy, and financially prosperous. That is not what this book is about.

That said, if I had to choose three words that best describe my life, they would be *A Blessed Life*. John 1:16 says, "From the fullness of his grace, we have all received one blessing after another" (NIV).[1] I live a blessed life because of who I am in

Jesus Christ.

This story is about life experiences: hardships, joys, and lessons learned. As a believer and follower of Jesus Christ, I've "received one blessing after another." Does this mean that life is without difficulties, trials, or problems of any kind? Absolutely not. Does this mean that all of my days are easy, full of happiness, or as others might deem, perfect? Of course not.

Suffering and joy, need and abundance, trial and peace go together, hand-in-hand in this adventure called life. As they do, we can see God's hand weaving together all of life's details. He is always there, showing Himself to us in ways we would never expect. Anticipating the unexpected, looking for God, and seeking Him should be our daily habit.

Being Blessed

What does it mean to be blessed? *Nelson's Illustrated Bible Dictionary* defines the word *bless* as "God's favor and goodness upon others."[2] God goes beyond material gifts to meet our spiritual, physical, mental, and emotional needs. God, with His divine grace, reaches down to bless us.

Why does God bless you? He blesses you because it gives Him pleasure. Let me say that again. God blesses you because it is pleasing to Him. God loves you.

We show love toward our children and our friends through our desire to do special things for them. When we do that, it gives us the best feeling. How much more pleasure God feels when He blesses us.

Jesus speaks about this in Matthew 7:9 and 11 when He says, "Or what man is there among you, when his son shall ask him for a loaf, will give him a stone?" He continues His encouragement by saying, "If you then, being evil, know how to give good gifts to your children, how much more shall your Father who is in heaven give what is good to those who ask Him!"

I like to imagine God receiving pleasure when He gives gifts to His children. Does He smile? Does He laugh? Does He share it with others around Him? Does He anticipate the moment He intends to pour out that blessing upon us?

What Is the Greatest Blessing We Can Receive?
Driving down a busy street, I glanced in the rearview mirror at my three-year-old son. Strapped safely in his car seat, David had his head turned to the empty seat next to him. I could hear him talking, but his words were hard to make out. He would pause as if in conversation, smile, laugh, and then begin talking again. After several minutes of this, curiosity got the better of me.

"David," I said, "to whom are you talking?"

He replied, "Jesus, Mommy."

Very surprised by his answer, I said, "But I don't see Jesus. Where is He?"

David patted the seat to his right and said with a huge smile, "Here, by me, Mommy."

All rules of the road went out the window at that point. I turned around to view the empty seat next to my son. David smiled at our invisible Guest and resumed his conversation.

In subsequent years, David recognized his need for Jesus. His nine-year-old explanation was very sincere and earnest. He knew that he had a hole in his heart, and Jesus was the only One who could fill it.

On another occasion, while standing in the kitchen preparing dinner for my family, my five-year-old daughter, Rachel, walked quietly into the room and head for the corner. Once there, she dropped to her knees and bowed her head so low she resembled a little ball.

After several minutes of watching her I finally asked, "Rachel, is everything okay, sweetheart?"

"Shh!" she said. "I need to finish. This is important."

Though startled by my daughter's reprimand, I allowed her to finish whatever she was doing. A few minutes later, Rachel stood up with a huge smile on her face. She skipped over to me and announced that she just asked Jesus to be her best friend and live in her heart. My heart filled with joy at her proclamation.

David and Rachel had figured out through basic, simple, childlike faith what it takes some people a lifetime to realize—they need Jesus. What about you? Do you need Jesus?

There are many things we receive from our Father in heaven, but none compare to the blessing of His Son, Jesus Christ. When Peter spoke to the men of Israel in the portico of Solomon, he declared that Jesus is the Christ. "For you first, God raised up His Servant, and sent Him to bless you by turning every one of you from your wicked ways" (Acts 3:26). Certainly, the gospel of Jesus Christ came first to the Jewish people. Praise God that the gospel message didn't stop there, but spread to the world. When Jesus is our Lord and Savior, we receive the incredible blessing of His presence in our lives, literally and permanently through His Holy Spirit. Those who accept God's gift of grace in His Son can know that they are profoundly blessed.

Do you see? God loves you so deeply that He sent Jesus for you. Every one has sinned, and there is nothing you can do to make yourself right before God. But God extends His grace through His Son, Jesus, who suffered, died on your behalf, and rose again. Turn from your sins, believe in Christ and what He did for you, and confess with your mouth Jesus Christ as Lord and Savior. Because Jesus died on the cross to take the penalty of your sin, His blood now covers your sin, so that when God looks at you, He sees His Son, Jesus, and that makes you blessed!

Romans 4:7-8 says, "Blessed are those whose lawless deeds have been forgiven, and whose sins have been covered. Blessed is the man whose sin the Lord will not take into account." If you don't know Jesus Christ as your Lord and Savior, I encourage you to pray, asking God to help you turn from your sin. Recognize that Jesus came to set you free from your wicked ways. Turn to Christ and receive Him into your life. Your time on Earth is short and will one day be over. None of us are guaranteed tomorrow. Believe in Jesus Christ today.

And Finally

As you read my stories and experiences, reflect on your own stories and look for the ways that you have experienced God's blessings. How does He work in the details of your life?

Thinking of God's hand in my own life, I'm reminded of Psalm 105. While reflecting on his experiences, the Psalmist encourages us to remember God's deeds, wonders, and marvels, by stating,

Oh give thanks to the Lord, call upon His name;
Make known His deeds among the peoples.
Sing to Him, sing praises to Him; speak of all His wonders.
Glory in His holy name; let the heart of those who seek the Lord be glad.
Seek the Lord and His strength; seek His face continually.
Remember His wonders which He has done, His marvels. . . .
 —Psalm 105:1–5a

What words come to mind as you read those verses? Read it again and see which words stand out to you. You might highlight *give thanks, call, make known, sing, praise, speak, marvel, be glad, seek,* or *remember.* These simple words become heartfelt experiences in the life of a believer in Jesus Christ.

I am full of gratitude for God's continual presence and marvel at the way He works. This book tells the story of my relationship with Jesus Christ, sharing the ways in which God has worked in the details of my life. God has blessed my life, and He can bless yours, too. As we journey together, let us remember the wonders that God has done and be reminded to seek Him, His strength, and His face continually. By doing so, I pray that you will discover the many ways that He blesses you every day.

How do you see yourself? Are you blessed? Perhaps you are, and you've just not realized it yet.

Jesus Christ is the ultimate channel of God's blessing.

Something to Consider
1. Who do you say Jesus is? Have you asked Him to forgive you of your sin?
2. Do you know where you will spend eternity?
3. If you know Jesus, have you told someone about Him? How has Jesus Christ made a difference in your life? Everyone has a story to tell.

Further Reflection
- Psalm 1:1–3
- Jeremiah 17:7–8
- 2 Corinthians 9:8
- Ephesians 1:3

CHAPTER 2
OUR SPIRITUAL HERITAGE

Great is the Lord, and highly to be praised;
And His greatness is unsearchable.
One generation shall praise Your works to another,
And shall declare Your mighty acts.
—*Psalm 145:3–4*

I don't remember a time in my life when I didn't know about Jesus. I learned about Him at church through Sunday school teachers, the pastor, and choir directors.

At home, my father and I had a weekly routine that I grew to cherish. When evening came, he would settle into his rocking chair. Bibles in hand, we would take turns reading from the passage of Scripture that Daddy had chosen that day. After reading, we would talk about what it meant and what it had to do with our lives.

Through these talks I became aware of my need for Jesus. When considering what life would be like without Jesus, it frightened me and made me cry. Daddy would hug me, tell me that I didn't need to be scared, and share with me a message of hope. I believed that Jesus was the Son of God, that He died on the cross to save me from sin, and that He rose again and lives today. I wanted to spend the rest of my life following Him.

At age ten, during a revival at our church, I walked down the long aisle to the front. There, I told the pastor that I believed in Jesus as my Lord and Savior and desired to follow Him in all my ways. The following week before the congregation, the words of the pastor rang out loud and strong, "I baptize you, Leigh Ann Kee, in the name of the Father, the Son, and the Holy Spirit." One woman wrote an encouraging letter in which she conveyed her happiness that I asked Jesus to come into my heart and be my Savior. She wrote, "Read your Bible and pray every day, and remember that Jesus is always close and will help you when you need Him."

As I went through junior high, high school, and college, my parents continued to encourage me in my faith. Through a treasure trove of letters and cards, my mother encouraged me to keep my eyes fixed on the Lord. When entering junior high school, she penned, "Remember to keep God in the center of your life and always ask for His guidance. We are so happy that God gave you to us. May God bless you and keep you. We love you very much."

During my freshman year of college, Mom's encouraging words lifted my spirits. "God will give you the strength you need, but you already know that firsthand. You have always looked to the Lord for your strength and guidance. He will see you through this time in your life." Later, she wrote to me in a card, "We will be thinking of you and praying for you for the days ahead. You do your part, and the Lord always does His."

I always knew that Mom and Dad prayed for me during my formative years, but only recently did I discover what they prayed for. During his long commutes to and from work, Daddy would ask God to bless my two sisters and me. He prayed for us to come to a saving faith in Jesus Christ, for our well-being and health, and for our education. He prayed for our future spouses—that God would lead us to whom He'd chosen for us, men who were kind and gentle. He asked that God would give him the wisdom and strength to let us go. My mother's prayers were much the same. I am deeply touched and grateful for the prayers of my parents.

The Faith of My Ancestors
My family has given me a precious gift that is not the norm in many households today. After years of taking this gift for granted, I've discovered that a rich spiritual heritage is truly to be treasured. I am a sixth-generation Christian on my father's side and a fourth-generation Christian on my mother's side. All of my living blood relatives are followers of Jesus Christ—my parents, sisters, nieces, nephews, aunts, uncles, cousins, and children. My husband, mother- and father-in-law, a sister-in-law, and brothers-in-law are as well. My son, David, and my daughter, Rachel, have the privilege of being seventh-generation believers.

My family members long ago passed the baton of faith in Jesus Christ to the next generation, who in turn passed that faith to their children. Psalm 78:5–7 speaks about this.

> *He commanded our fathers*
> *That they should teach them to their children,*
> *That the generation to come might know, even the children*
> *yet to be born,*
> *That they may arise and tell them to their children,*
> *That they should put their confidence in God.*

It is through the faithfulness of my ancestors that so many have discovered a saving relationship with our Savior and God. Generation after generation loved Jesus Christ, shared with their children and grandchildren the love of God, and modeled a life of commitment to reading the Bible and praying.

My grandmother Mama Kee lived one block from her grandmother and would often go there to talk about the Lord. My great-grandfather was known to read his Bible while sitting on the front porch of his home. My grandparents loved taking my family to church during our visits. They would talk about Jesus and the faith they had in Him. The beautiful thing about their faith was that it transcended Sundays to all aspects of their lives. They followed Jesus Christ not just at church, but everywhere they went.

My father spent hours talking with his mother about spiritual issues—faith, the Bible, and prophecy. Because of that, he developed a passion for the Bible and read it voraciously until illness in his later years took that ability away. My mother tells stories of faith from her childhood. Since the town she grew up in was so small, they went to all of the revivals, regardless of denomination. She heard Baptist, Methodist, and Church of Christ preachers all faithfully preach the gospel.

Because both of my parents grew up in the church and heard about Jesus from childhood, it's not surprising that they both asked Jesus into their hearts at the age of nine. When they were joined in marriage, they dedicated their lives, their home, and their children to the Lord.

Building a Spiritual Heritage

One generation shall praise Your works to another,
And shall declare Your mighty acts.
On the glorious splendor of Your majesty
And on Your wonderful works, I will meditate.
Men shall speak of the power of Your awesome acts,
And I will tell of Your greatness.
They shall eagerly utter the memory of Your abundant goodness
And will shout joyfully of Your righteousness.
—Psalm 145:4–7

A heritage, according to Jim Weidmann, is the "spiritual, emotional, and social legacy a child receives—for good or for bad."[3] Everyone has a heritage of some kind. Some may relate to my personal experiences and upbringing. Others may feel short-changed in this area. If you find yourself in the latter group, don't be discouraged about the past, but seek ways to build a better heritage for future generations.

Two of my friends faced this challenge. Growing up in unstable home environments that were void of Christian teaching, my friends didn't seek Christ until well into their adult years. They then made a choice to follow Christ and leave a better heritage for their own children than the one they inherited.

What legacy will live on after you're gone? If you are a parent, you have a responsibility to provide a spiritual heritage for your children. Regardless of the choices your children make when they are older, you're responsible for how you raise them and what you teach them about the Lord.

How do you do this?

Teach and instruct children in the ways of God. Weave the Word of God into your daily conversations and activities. As suggested in Deuteronomy 6:7, talk about the things of God when you are seated, when you stand, when you walk, and when you lie down. If you don't know how to do this, then consider the advice of pastor and author Charles Stanley. "Find out what your children are interested in, and then talk about those things and weave the truths of God into what you discuss. That is the way to hand down your faith."[4]

Our children like hiking in the mountains. As we enjoy being outdoors, we talk with our kids about the creativity of our God, looking for the beautiful things He has made in nature—the variety of leaves, the majesty of the mountains, the sound of the waterfall, and the expanse of the sky. As our children have gotten older, those simple childhood conversations have become more complex, with discussions on technology, friends, music, movies, books, and the latest news headlines.

As I write this, my husband and I have begun yet a new stage with our son and daughter. Now conversations are about relationships, theology, college, graduate school, and careers. By directing them to God's Word and His ways, we try to teach them how to discern and make wise, godly decisions. We rejoice when we see our children follow God's precepts, but we also know that the years of directly influencing them are coming to an end as they make their faith their own.

Create spiritual milestones and traditions. Growing up in my home, Christmas Eve was very important. Before heading to bed, we would gather as a family, and my father would tell us about the birth of Jesus from Luke 2. Sitting in his rocking chair, he read from the large, red family Bible: "Now it came about in those days that a decree went out from Caesar Augustus...."

Following Daddy's closing prayer, we would sing our favorite Christmas songs before getting ready for bed. Those precious traditions have now been implemented in my own family. Whether on birthdays, holidays, or vacations, use these special times to create faith memories for your children.

Spend time with your children and talk with them. Then, listen to them—really listen. Tell them your life stories and what you learned from them. Many of my life experiences were bedtime stories that my children heard repeatedly. You could give your children everything under the sun, but the one thing they really desire is your time.

Model Christ's love to your children. Our children learn from our example. That can be scary! Sometimes our kids pick up things from us that we would rather they didn't, such as complaining, arguing, and cursing. As parents, we have the privilege of setting godly examples for these young lives entrusted to us. We not only have to purpose to do these things, but we must be consistent in doing them.

Now for parents with grown children and those who are grandparents, what legacy will live on after you're gone? Give priority to relationships with your adult children and your grandchildren. Maybe you weren't a Christian when your children were young, but you are now. It's never too late to set a good example and pray for those you love. Maybe your grandchildren don't live close to you. But you can influence their lives through encouraging words, cards, letters, telephone calls, texts, and visits. Teach and model through your words and actions what it means to love Jesus and to live for Him.

Those who have no children may wonder how they can live a life that will be remembered well. What kind of legacy will you leave behind? You may not have children, but if you're a member of a community of faith, you have a responsibility to encourage parents as they raise their children. Further, you can speak directly into children's lives by sharing with them the truths of God's Word. Communicate the things that are important to you, especially things of faith. Outside of church, create time to be with family and friends. Whether interacting with a child or another adult, pass the baton of faith to others through your words and actions.

If you're a first generation Christian, don't be discouraged or troubled. Understand the impact that you can make for Jesus Christ on those following you. You can be the first generation to pass that faith on, and you may even experience the blessing of seeing your older relatives come to faith.

Oh, the spiritual blessings you have received by believing in the death and resurrection of Jesus Christ! Through His divine gift, you have life, salvation, forgiveness, adoption, the indwelling of the Holy Spirit, and so much more. "I pray that the eyes of your heart may be enlightened, so that you may know what is the hope of His calling, what are the riches of the glory of His inheritance in the saints, and what is the surpassing greatness of His power toward us who believe" (Ephesians 1:18–19). You may not have a spiritual heritage to build upon, but you have the strongest foundation there is—Jesus Christ. He is sufficient.

When Jesus is truly Lord in your family, it will influence everything you do, from the way you decorate your house to the way you spend your summer vacation. What books do you read? What music do you listen to? What hangs on your walls? What do you watch on television? What websites are you viewing? Following Christ is a way of life that is lived 24/7, not just on Sundays at church. May you and your family echo the words of Joshua when he boldly proclaimed, "As for me and my house, we will serve the Lord" (Joshua 24:15).

Our spiritual heritage is a channel of God's blessing.

Something to Consider
1. Name three ways you can be diligent and consistent in living a life of faith.
2. What is most important to you? What can you pass on as an example for others?
3. What will those closest to you remember about you when you're gone? What would you like them to remember about you? What are some changes for the better that you might make?

Further Reflection
- Deuteronomy 4:9
- Deuteronomy 6:4–9
- Psalm 78:5–7
- 2 Timothy 1:5; 3:14–15

CHAPTER 3
EXPERIENCING ANGELS

*For He will give His angels charge concerning you,
To guard you in all your ways.*
—*Psalm 91:11*

"I've seen an angel!" Make that comment in a room full of people, and you'll stop all other conversations. You will either be met with curiosity or with skepticism—curiosity, because people are genuinely interested in things that are mysterious; skepticism, because people have difficulty believing in the supernatural.

Angels are real beings created by God. Colossians 1:16 tells us, "For by Him all things were created, both in the heavens and on earth, visible and invisible, whether thrones or dominions or rulers or authorities—all things have been created by Him and for Him." We also know from Scripture that angels are ministering spirits sent to serve those who will inherit salvation (Hebrews 1:14). They have a job to do—to serve those who follow Jesus Christ, watching over and guarding them. I wholeheartedly agree with Billy Graham's view on angels: "I believe in angels because the Bible says there are angels; and I believe the Bible to be the true Word of God."⁵

Growing up, I was told fascinating stories about family members who saw or experienced the presence of angels.

My grandfather Papa Clewis was rushed to a hospital after suffering a heart attack. Papa, being near death, had his heart shocked back into a normal rhythm by the attending doctors. Once conscious and with family gathered by his bedside, he told them that as the doctors worked on him, he had a vision of an angel. In this vision, Papa was walking down the side of a road. He saw a bright light and a man in a long, white robe. Smiling at my grandfather, the man told him, "Scott, I'm not ready for you yet. You need to go back."

Mama Kee was at a hospital for a series of tests to determine if she had cancer. Mama Kee did not like needles, and as a true prayer warrior, she told God how frightened she was before going in for a needle-biopsy of her liver. During the biopsy, she was in pain, but at the foot of the examination table stood an angel who brought her great comfort.

One evening my aunt, grandparents, and young cousin were driving back to their hometown when their car broke down. Pulling off to the side of the highway, their concern grew as the sun set and the sky turned dark. A broken down car, the arrival of dusk, a child, and two aging parents all led to Aunt Nancy's sense of urgency for help. Knowing her true source of help, Aunt Nancy turned to God in prayer.

Not long after telling God of her need, a man drove up to see if he could assist them. When asked if he happened to be a car mechanic, he replied, "Yes, as a matter of fact, I am." After determining the problem, the stranger knew precisely how to repair their car. As my aunt explained to me, "It was not a simple fix. This man had the exact knowledge on how to make the repairs; he even had the correct tools in his car."

Seeing the mechanic as a direct answer to her prayer, she repeatedly told him that she knew he was an angel sent by

God. Upon finishing his repairs, the man refused to accept any money in return. Aunt Nancy insisted that he tell her his name and where he worked, so that she could properly pay him and speak a good word on his behalf. He told her his name was Willie Nelson, and he was employed by Trinity Industries. He then went on his way.

Aunt Nancy felt he just picked that name out of the blue, because he was definitely not the country music legend Willie Nelson. The next day, she called the Dallas-based Trinity Industries and inquired about the mechanic. They explained that no one by that name worked there. This was just what my aunt expected to hear. That man was no man. He was an angel sent to help my loved ones in their distress.

In the midst of this event, did you notice God's sense of humor? Perhaps this "man" was employed at Trinity Industries—the heavenly branch!

My own encounter with an angel happened when I was in high school, as my parents and I drove on a desolate New Mexico highway. The mountains in the distance were to the west, but the road was pancake flat. You could see for miles, and no cars were on the road except ours. As we drove across the prairie that afternoon, the weather became stormy, the heavy rains and hail making it difficult for my father to drive.

Just the week before, my family spent several hours in a courthouse basement in Armstrong County in Texas because of a tornado sighting. On this empty highway, there was no place to take cover, so we continued driving. Seated in the backseat, scared to death, I prayed, "God, help us! I'm so frightened. Please protect us."

Moments after praying, I looked out the side passenger window and saw a small, white pickup truck driving beside us. The man driving had dark hair, a beard, and a mustache. Dressed in a white button-down dress shirt, he looked directly at me and smiled. As I looked back and returned the smile, a feeling of peace came over me. Everything was going to be all right.

After he drove ahead of our car, I turned to check the storm clouds behind me. When I looked to see how far the truck was in front of us, it was gone. I scanned the road for miles, but the truck wasn't there. I asked my parents where the white truck turned off of the road. They looked puzzled. After describing the truck to them, my father explained that we'd been the only car on the road for some time. I knew an angel had comforted and encouraged me with the peace of Jesus Christ.

Some will believe these angel encounters because they have stories of their own to tell. Others will approach the idea of angels with great skepticism, and that's understandable. The supernatural is often difficult to wrap our mind around. Why? Because, as Graham suggests, it's not natural and is beyond the way we work and function as human beings.

> The subject of angels will be of great comfort and inspiration to believers in God—and a challenge to unbelievers to believe. . . . Those who take the Bible at full value cannot discount the subject of angels as speculation or hollow conjecture. After all, the Scriptures mention their existence almost three hundred times.[6]

Whether we see them or not, there is a vast host of angels that God has created with the purpose of accomplishing His work in this world.

Let me leave you with one more thought from Billy Graham. "Angels are watching; they mark our path. They superintend the events of our lives and protect the interest of the Lord God, always working to promote His plans and to bring about His highest will for us."[7] We're so important to God that He assigns His angels to watch over us.

Ministering angels are a channel of God's blessing.

Something to Consider
1. How do you respond to someone who claims to have seen an angel?
2. Have you ever had an experience with an angel?
3. God assigns His angels to watch over you. As a Christian, what are your thoughts on that?

Further Reflection
- Psalm 34:7
- Psalm 91:11–12
- Acts 12:7–10
- Hebrews 13:2

CHAPTER 4

HIS GRACE IS SUFFICIENT FOR ME

When you hear the word *obstacle*, what comes to mind? It may bring images of an obstacle course in which a runner makes his way through a series of hurdles, fences, walls, or ditches. Or you may think of something blocking your path, such as a fallen tree in the road. Maybe your definition is anything impeding progress or achievement. For some, this word takes them to a difficult time. For two and a half years, I faced a serious obstacle that prevented me from living the life of freedom God intended.

It was February of 1985, and I was on a stage in San Antonio, Texas, at the Convention Center Theater in front of a large audience of music directors, parents, and students. During my senior year in high school, our symphonic band was awarded the title of Texas State Honor Band. This was an impressive achievement, and I was excited to be performing before many musicians. My chair at the end of the row in the French horn section placed me directly in front of the audience. I don't recall playing a note during the entire concert, but I do remember my heart pounding, being short of breath, feeling dizzy, and sensing that I was losing control. I was in the grips of performance anxiety.

I wish that was the only time panic overwhelmed reason, but it was not. During the remainder of my senior year in high school and my freshman year in college, this condition escalated into a serious panic disorder. My choice of music education/vocal major didn't help, as one of the requirements of the degree was to perform numerous times throughout the semester. With each concert, I endured the same horrible experience as I did in San Antonio.

By my sophomore year, the attacks were so frequent and frightening that they began to interfere with my daily activities. The worst was going to the mall. It was difficult to walk in such an open space with crowds of people surrounding me. What if I passed out and fell? What would happen then? Suffering in silence became a way of life, for to share this with anyone might mean I was crazy. I was an agoraphobic, someone who fears public places.

My parents weren't aware of my condition—I hid it well. In March of 1987, I experienced an attack while driving home in fast-moving traffic on the interstate in downtown Dallas. City workers had just repaved the roads, so the tires made a shrill sound on the new concrete. In my panic-driven mind, the whistling became the sound of angels ready to take me home. Anxiety took over. I was hyperventilating, my heart pounding, body numbing, and everything spinning. In a feeble attempt at prayer, only two words came out: "Help me!"

Through grace, God brought me to my parents' house. Unable to hide what had happened, I told them about the two years of panic attacks and what it felt like enduring deep fear. Deeply concerned, my parents discussed options for getting me help. We decided to turn to a university Christian counselor available to students attending Baylor University.

At the end of that weekend, God enabled me to make the drive back to Waco for classes. Alone in my apartment, I experienced a turning point in my life.

Throwing myself prostrate on the floor for a lengthy time, I cried out to God. "Lord," I said, "if You want to use my life in any way, please remove this burden from me. I cannot function like this. Help me, God!"

Growing up as a believer in Jesus Christ, I knew He was my Savior. But on that day, I began to learn what it meant to allow Him to be my Lord. Absolute surrender was required— the giving up of my will for His. Andrew Murray says, "If our hearts are willing for this kind of commitment, there is no limit to what God will do for us or to the blessing that will follow in our lives."[8] God heard my prayer; I have not had a panic attack since that day. My need to see a counselor was no longer necessary.

Before continuing, let me add a cautionary note. If you are suffering from panic attacks, pray, for God hears your prayers. At the same time, I do not want to discourage anyone from seeking professional help. I do not doubt the healing power of God, but know that God's healing often comes through the skilled expertise of doctors, counselors, and pastors.

God removed panic attacks from my life on that night in my apartment. However, it took many years to learn what blessings would come from those two painful years.

How can we find great good in the face of obstacles in our lives? Let me share some of the blessings that are true for all believers. Mind you, these are not new ideas. They're straight from Scripture. These verses can lead you to freedom in life, especially when facing obstacles.

1. When you are weak, rely on God's power, strength, and grace to carry you.

> *And He said to me, "My grace is sufficient for you, for power is perfected in weakness." Most gladly, therefore, I*

> *will rather boast about my weaknesses, that the power of Christ may dwell in me.*
>
> —*2 Corinthians 12:9*

When my children were young, they would make F.R.O.G. (Fully Rely On God) bracelets at church. They would run up to me, hold out their wrists, and announce how they wanted to fully rely on God. We must learn to rely fully on God in the good times, so that when the bad times come, we're used to depending on Him. When obstacles come your way, admit that you're weak and in need of God's grace.

When I stand before a crowd to speak or sing, this encouraging verse runs through my mind. Nervousness still occurs, especially when singing before a crowd, but when I pray about it and tell God my feelings, He steps in and helps me every time.

Maybe you're thinking that your problem is too big, that there is no way God could ever overcome your obstacle. Rick Warren, in his book *The Purpose Driven Life*, made a comment that has stuck with me. "God is never limited by our limitations."[9] There is nothing too difficult for Him! God can do the impossible in your life; He did in mine.

2. Sometimes God allows us to have a "thorn in the flesh."

> *[T]here was given me a thorn in the flesh, a messenger of Satan to buffet me—to keep me from exalting myself! Concerning this I entreated the Lord three times that it might depart from me.*
>
> —*2 Corinthians 12:7–8*

You may be thinking, "What? How can a thorn in the flesh possibly be a blessing?" Like Paul in the verse above, I've pleaded with God to remove any feelings of anxiousness when performing. Playing and singing at the piano in my home is a very comfortable environment, but place me in a formal setting to perform, and the tension builds.

One blessing is that a thorn in the flesh may keep us from thinking too highly of our abilities. It's hard to exalt ourselves when we're on our hands and knees before God, fully relying on Him to equip us.

Did you notice the second blessing? We depend on God, relying on Him for His power, strength, and grace. He has healed me from panic attacks, but any anxiousness I experience causes me to lean completely on God and remember His past mercy.

The third blessing is that each time we see God working in these weak areas, we become more confident. If He got us through that last obstacle, then He will be there for us during the next one. If you have a thorn in the flesh and see it only as a hindrance, ask God to show you how it might actually be a blessing.

3. Use your obstacle to encourage others who may be going through the same thing.

> *Blessed be the God and Father of our Lord Jesus Christ, the Father of mercies and God of all comfort, who comforts us in all our affliction so that we may be able to comfort those who are in any affliction with the comfort with which we ourselves are comforted by God.*
> —2 Corinthians 1:3–4

Repeatedly, people have told me about their struggles with panic attacks. Having experienced them firsthand, I can move beyond sympathy to empathy. It encourages another person when you can look at them and say, "I know something about that, because I've been there." It's a blessing to help and comfort others.

One woman's panic attacks interfered with her job and kept her up through the night. When she talked to people about her problem, they would be sympathetic, but sometimes impatient, as if thinking, "Get over it." At church one evening, I asked how she was doing and let her talk without saying a word about my own past experiences. Right before the service began, I told her that we should get together and visit because I knew what she was experiencing; I, too, had suffered panic attacks for two years. Relief flooded her face.

Share with others your experiences with obstacles. There may be someone who needs to hear from you.

4. There is freedom in Jesus Christ. When we belong to Him, we are no longer held captive by our fears and worries.

For God has not given us a spirit of timidity, but of power and love and discipline."
—2 Timothy 1:7

Some years ago, while preparing to give a talk to a large group at a weekend retreat, the butterflies in my stomach went into full flight. Needing a quiet space to pull myself together, I headed to the empty chapel to tell God my troubled thoughts. Having prayed many Scriptures dealing with anxiety and anticipating that His grace would be sufficient for me, I asked God to give me something else from Scripture to hang on to.

Flipping through the pages of my open Bible, my eyes fell on 2 Timothy 1:7. It was like God was speaking out loud saying, *Leigh Ann, I have not given you a spirit of fear, but of power and of love and of a sound mind.* That verse was enough, a reminder that He is in control.

What great freedom we can experience when we belong to Jesus Christ. We are no longer bound by our fears and worries;

He replaces those old thoughts with a new way of thinking. When your mind goes into overdrive, full of fear and worry, take those thoughts to Jesus. Pray 2 Corinthians 10:5: "…we are taking every thought captive to the obedience of Christ."

Tell Him, "Lord, I'm afraid. But I know that you haven't given me a spirit of fear. Take captive the fearful thoughts that I am having to the obedience of Christ."

Prayer brings freedom from the fears and worries that bind us.

What are your obstacles? What are you struggling with right now? It might be fears or worries, an illness or job loss. Maybe it's a wayward child or a painful memory. Whatever the obstacle is, whatever weakness you're struggling with, know that God's grace is sufficient for you. When you turn to Him and admit your weaknesses, He is able to carry and bless you at the same time. Do you want God to demonstrate His power in your life? Then it's okay to be weak. God loves to work in our weakness.

Obstacles are a channel of God's blessing.

Something to Consider
1. Do you see your obstacles or weaknesses as a hindrance? List them on paper. Commit to pray over these, asking God what blessings might be hidden in them.
2. Where can you use your own life experience to encourage someone who is struggling?
3. What fears and worries do you need to take to Jesus? Once you lay them at His feet, you do not need to pick them up again!

Further Reflection
- Psalm 138:3
- Isaiah 40:28–31
- 2 Corinthians 1:3–4
- 2 Corinthians 12:7–10

CHAPTER 5
A LOVE STORY

As I write this, there is a melancholy tug in my heart. My husband is preparing to leave for a three-week trip to Great Britain, where he will be teaching history to a large group of Lee University students.

I can't help but recall how the two of us met and grew to know each other over five weeks in a foreign country. God wrote a beautiful story for us—one that I could not have dreamed up had I tried.

A Childhood Dream
As a young girl, I thought about growing up and marrying the man that God had chosen for me. A vivid imagination played out the entire scene: our first meeting and our conversations over time eventually leading to a much-desired proposal. Tucked into my bed at night, dreams of my wedding day would complete the drama, as the orchestra performed, Daddy walked me down the aisle whispering words of wisdom into my ear, and a long veil flowed behind me, just like Maria's veil in *The Sound of Music*.

During my freshman year at Baylor University, I was introduced to a young man whom I would date for almost two years. Wondering if this relationship would turn into something more serious, I turned to my father for wisdom and the answer to my recurring question, "How will I know if he is the right man for me, the one God has chosen?" Daddy smiled and repeated the same response every time, "You'll just know. When you meet a man who cares for you more than he cares for himself, you'll know. It will be right." It turned out that this young man didn't meet Daddy's criteria, and we broke up.

Nursing a broken heart, I surrendered my will and asked God to take over and find the man I was to marry. Regardless of what God decided, He could be trusted. Little did I know that God was already at work in the midst of my circumstances. Long ago, He laid out a course of events for me. His providential hand was moving. God would bring healing to my heart and maneuver me into a place where I would listen to Him.

Ireland
At the end of my sophomore year, I received a letter from the dean of the music school inviting me to participate in a program called Baylor in the British Isles. After much consideration and discussion with my parents, I accepted the invitation and enrolled in the class, Music and Society. This particular trip was intriguing—the chance to travel overseas for the first time, exciting musical opportunities, and a completely new experience with people I'd never met.

On July 9, 1987, I traveled with more than fifty students to Shannon, Ireland. Upon arrival, we checked into the Two Mile Inn in Limerick with just enough time to freshen up and board the coaches headed to Bunratty Castle for a medieval banquet.

Coming into the castle courtyard that evening, we were greeted by a kilted Irishman playing a tune on his whistle. He led us into a large hall full of long oak tables set for a meal. The bench seats and candles reflected the banqueting style of the era, and we dined on a four-course meal of traditional Irish dishes.

A man carrying a large platter announced that one item on the menu had a story. Hidden in our loaves of bread was a small ring, signifying an impending romance and marriage. As the slices of bread were passed from table to table, students began tearing through their bread to see if they held the prize. Within my piece, I discovered a small metal band wrapped carefully in parchment paper. As people congratulated me on my future romance and marriage, I laughed and thought to myself, "Not a chance. I did not come on this trip to meet a guy."

Turning my attention to the music and Irish dancers, the ring sat tucked into the corner of my pocket. Lying in bed later that night and turning the little band over and over in my fingers, I ended my day with a short prayer, "Lord, wouldn't that be neat if it really worked?"

God's Providential Hand
After breakfast the next morning, we settled on the coach for a drive through the Irish countryside of rolling hills carpeted with green grass and spotted with flocks of sheep. After several hours of travel, we stopped in the fishing village of Dingle in southwest Ireland.

I followed a small group to John Silver's Seafood Restaurant (not Long John Silver's!). Seated around the table were seven people who began to make introductions to one another, myself included. A guy named John Coats was sitting across from me, so I visited with him the most. As we talked, a list of comparisons was made: he was studying history, I was studying music; he was in a fraternity, I chose not to participate in Greek life; he has the drawl of a Texan, I spoke with the precision of one who studied vocal diction. We were very different, yet were drawn to one another.

As we traveled through Ireland, I saw more of John. Touring Kilkenny Castle was especially memorable. Our elderly tour guide must have known every minute detail of the castle. As he carefully and painstakingly described each carving on the massive marble fireplace, I found my way over to a large window from where I could view the lovely gardens. The flowers were attractive, but quietly standing beside me was a far more appealing figure—John. He invited me to skip the remainder of the tour and join him for a walk in the gardens. How could I pass that up?

As we walked near the rose beds, we talked about who we were and where we grew up. While the tour slowly wound through the castle, we found ourselves on the far end of the immense manicured lawns, so far that when the coach blew its horn, we had to run to catch our ride.

The next day, we were given the afternoon to explore Dublin on our own. John and I headed off to see the sights in this sprawling city. After walking several miles, we came to John's Lane Augustinian Church. The moment we walked into this hidden gem, I sensed the Holy Spirit's presence. Looking at John, I was deeply touched by his posture. He stood with his head slightly raised and his eyes closed as if praying. His quiet reverence suggested he was a man of faith.

We then walked through the old narrow streets until we came to the beautiful Cathedral of Holy Trinity. This ornate cathedral, commonly called Christ Church, is one of Dublin's oldest buildings, dating back to the eleventh century. On the grounds are gardens and a grassy park with a fountain in the center of it.

John and I sat in that park for hours, talking, learning new things about each other, and laughing as a little dog playfully swiped the shoe of his owner. Everything was just right—beautiful weather, an awe-inspiring cathedral, and delightful company. I remember thinking, "Here I am in a foreign country talking with a handsome young man. Can this really be happening to me?"

England
After a week in Ireland, we traveled to London, where we settled into our home for the remainder of the trip: the 800-year-old Westminster School, next to the world-famous Westminster Abbey in the heart of London. To reach the school, we walked through a series of courtyards. First, we left busy Victoria Street and entered the Dean's Yard, which had an expansive grassy lawn enclosed on all four sides by old four-story brick buildings. We then passed through a small, gated archway into the intimate, paved Little Dean's Yard, where dormitories, gardens, and cloisters were hidden from the main street outside. It was a fascinating, private world.

Equally wonderful was the friendship developing between John and me. On our first day in London, we walked hand in hand past St. James Park, Buckingham Palace, and Big Ben, before arriving at the Thames River to watch the sunset. Returning to our dorms at Westminster School, a group of bagpipers practiced in a nearby building, as John kissed me by the big red mailbox in the courtyard. A perfect end to a wonderful day.

Over four weeks in England, John and I went to the British Museum and the National Gallery of Art, took a day trip with some of our new friends to the beach in Bournemouth, picnicked in Regent's Park, and visited the London Zoo. There was something special about getting to know John in a foreign country—it removed the barriers of college life, such as conflicting schedules, our own circle of friends, John's fraternity, and my music school. Without the distractions of our normal routines, we focused on one another (and our studies of course!).

Before heading back to the United States, John planned a surprise day trip for the two of us. One morning after breakfast, we took a train to the market town of Ely. Free from crowds of tourists, Ely boasted beautiful green parks, houses adorned with thatched roofs and flower gardens, and small, quaint shops. Looming over the town was the tower of Ely Cathedral.

Wonderful memories were made that day: walking through the cathedral, sharing a picnic lunch, and watching a wedding exit the parish church accompanied by the peal of bells. After returning to London, we headed out for a concert of Handel's *Water Music* and then to see fireworks near the Barbican Center. What a day!

Talking to my parents late that night, I shared my thoughts about John. "This cannot end," I said. "Anything this romantic just cannot end!"

A Childhood Dream Comes True
When we got back to Baylor University, we began dating. I learned about the world of fraternities, and John learned the intricacies of the music school. One evening, after dinner at my apartment, I broached the subject that would determine if our relationship would continue. I'd resolved years before that any romantic relationship hinged on the answer to one question.

"John, what do you think about Jesus Christ?"

"Well, Jesus Christ is my Lord and my Savior," he said sincerely. "Why don't you tell me what you think about Him?"

I answered the same. We then talked about our faith and being raised in Christian homes.

I never dated another person after meeting John. The more time we spent together, the more comfortable we became with each other. It was clear that we were headed toward marriage. Week after week was spent anticipating when John would propose to me, but after several months of waiting, I stopped trying to figure things out. In September of 1989, when I least expected it, John surprised me. After dinner, I sat down as John pulled out a small box and asked me to marry him.

On May 19, 1990, John and I entered into the covenant of marriage before God and all our family and friends. Our wedding day was all I had hoped and dreamed of and more. There was no orchestra, but I was very content with the piano, organ, and string quartet. My father didn't whisper words of wisdom in my ear, but rather whispered words that make me smile to this day. And I did wear the long cathedral-length veil, just like Maria in *The Sound of Music*. It was a beautiful day. My childhood dream come true.

Occasionally, I still pull out the little ring found in the Irish bread, a fun trinket that God used to usher romance and marriage into my life. God chose a husband for me who is an answer to my prayers. John Coats has truly captured my heart.

An Even Greater Love Story

You've read how I met my husband, the lover of my heart. There are many things he can do, but there comes a point where he reaches his limitations. It would be unfair to expect certain things from John that only God can provide.

My husband is strong, but only God can be my Strength. My husband is a confident man, but only God can be my Rock. My husband knows me intimately, but only God can search and examine my heart and mind. My husband can give me words of comfort, but only God can give me peace that surpasses understanding. My husband tries to protect me from harm and difficulties, but only God can save my soul.

Let me tell you about a love that is even greater than my husband's; it involves the Lover of my soul, Jesus Christ. I have known Him for a long time, but He has known me much longer. This love relationship was initiated by God before my birth—He knew me and loved me before the creation of the world.

To have the God of all creation pursue and be attracted to us is a mystery. There is nothing that we do or can ever do that deserves that kind of divine love, yet He is drawn to us. Why does the Desirable One seek the undesirable? The answer lies with Him. 1 John 4:8 says, "God is love." He is the author of love; He Himself is love.

This book demonstrates the relationship I have with my Lord. Woven into the words of each chapter, God continually calls me to Himself. He passionately woos and courts, desiring to have all of me, not just a portion. It's a relationship. Think of the things people do in a relationship. They listen, talk, laugh, cry, dance, solve problems, tell secrets, and are still. Those same things are done in relationship with God Himself.

Just like the moments I cherish with my earthly husband, I can recall precious memories with my heavenly Beloved.

- While working in my garden, enjoying the intricacies of a rose and its scent, I sensed God saying, *Do you like it? I'm glad it gives you pleasure.* I often feel God's presence when I tend to His flowers.

- When playing the piano and singing, I imagine Jesus outside the window leaning on the tree listening. Praising and worshiping Him through music, I feel as if Jesus is there. It would be a wonderful thing to have my sight opened to the spiritual realm to physically see the One being worshiped.

- One day while making pralines and listening to some upbeat music about Jesus, I began to dance, with one arm raised to Him and the other stirring the praline mixture in soft-boil stage. (Cooks know that it's crucial to keep stirring!) I just knew that God was smiling and that we were laughing together.

- Late at night while lying in bed, my heart was troubled about a strained relationship with someone I loved. While

talking to Jesus about it, I physically felt His blanket of peace cover me.
- Several times while praying, a dove has flown down singing its comforting song. It was as if God was saying, *I am here, Leigh Ann, and I've been listening to you.*
- When being selfish with my time, God interjects His questions into my thoughts. *Where have you been? Come back to me. I miss you, Leigh Ann.* Upon returning to God and confessing my sin, I can sense the sweet restoration of our relationship.

These are intimate recollections between my Savior and me. While I cannot see and touch Him like I can my husband, John, His presence is often felt or sensed; sometimes, I hear His Spirit speak to my spirit. You may wonder how God pursues you. Here are five ways you can experience God's pursuit.

1. God pursues you through Scripture.
The Bible is the ultimate love story. This love story is not just my story, but it can be your story, too. The Bible tells us of God's great love for you and me and how He desires to have a relationship with us through His Son, Jesus Christ. Do you need to hear God tell how much He loves you? May these words from Scripture stir your heart and awaken your soul to how much you are loved!

> *For God so loved the world that He gave His only begotten Son, that whoever believes in Him should not perish, but have eternal life. For God did not send the Son into the world to judge the world, but that the world should be saved through Him.*
> —*John 3:16–17*

The Lord your God is in your midst,
A victorious warrior.
He will exult over you with joy,
He will be quiet in His love,
He will rejoice over you with shouts of joy.
—Zephaniah 3:17

The Lord appeared to him from afar, saying,
"I have loved you with an everlasting love;
Therefore I have drawn you with lovingkindness."
—Jeremiah 31:3

But God, being rich in mercy, because of His great love with which He loved us, even when we were dead in our transgressions, made us alive together with Christ (by grace you have been saved), and raised us up with Him, and seated us with Him in the heavenly places, in Christ Jesus, in order that in the ages to come He might show the surpassing riches of His grace in kindness toward us in Christ Jesus.
—Ephesians 2:4–7

By this the love of God was manifested in us, that God has sent His only begotten Son into the world so that we might live through Him. In this is love, not that we loved God, but that He loved us and sent His Son to be the propitiation for our sins.
—1 John 4:9–10

2. God pursues you through other people.
Oftentimes, God gets our attention through the most unexpected people—a child, an elderly person, or a neighbor. One of the most powerful experiences of God's presence was His calling me to Himself through the taped words of the late Dr. S.M. Lockridge, a well-known pastor. Hearing the spoken

words of his sermon "That's My King" invoked in me an intense longing for my Savior.[10]

3. God pursues you through His creation.
When you look around, you can see the fingerprints of God everywhere—the mountains, the sunsets, the cornfields, the trees. God often loves on me when I'm working in my garden, tending to His creation. Stand on a beach and take in the magnitude and power displayed in the water. The One who created that is the same One who desires you.

4. God pursues you through song.
You can listen to the words of a hymn or a praise chorus, only to hear those very words ringing out to your soul. God is wooing you through those lyrics, wanting you to come to Him.

5. God pursues you through gifts.
His spiritual riches are abundant, but one gift stands before all others—the cross. His love is proven forever at the cross of Jesus. God loves you. He sent His Son to become a man, live the life you couldn't, and then to suffer and die on the cross. The good news is that Jesus rose from the dead and lives today, calling you to Himself. God did this for you, so that by believing in His Son, you could spend eternity with Him. That is a precious gift.

In an attempt to define God's love, J.I. Packer wrote, "God's love is an exercise of his goodness toward individual sinners whereby, having identified himself with their welfare, he has given his Son to be their Savior, and now brings them to know and enjoy him in a covenant relation."[11] God wants you to know and enjoy Him in a covenant relationship.

What is a covenant? Packer explains that "a covenant relation is one in which two parties are permanently pledged to each other in mutual service and dependence (example: marriage). A covenant promise is one by which a covenant relation is set up (example: marriage vows)."[12] I entered into the covenant of marriage with my husband, John; I entered into a similar relationship with my Lord. You, too, can have that same intimate relationship with God.

In the Bible, God uses the imagery of marriage over and over again. When you're a follower of Jesus Christ, you become part of the church, the body of Christ. Jesus often refers to the church as His bride; that makes Him the bridegroom. Pastor Max Anders describes the outcome of the bride being united to the bridegroom.

> The vows are given, and the bride is united to the groom. The two become one. That is the destiny of Christians. Someday in heaven we will be honored as no bride on earth has ever been honored. To think that Jesus would honor us! It is we who should honor Him, and yet a ceremony confirming His marriage to us is conducted in heaven. The apostle John wrote, "Hallelujah! For the Lord our God, the Almighty, reigns. Let us rejoice and be glad and give the glory to Him, for the marriage of the Lamb has come and His bride has made herself ready.... Blessed are those who are invited to the marriage supper of the Lamb" (Revelation 19:6, 7, 9, NASB). Are these not amazing pictures? You are the body of Christ. You are the temple of God in the Spirit. You are the bride of Christ. As the body, you have a task, you are gifted. As a building, you belong, you are possessed and indwelt by the living God, you reflect His glory. As a bride, you are honored, you are owned, you are glorified. By whom? Of all persons, by Jesus![13]

You've read about two love stories in this chapter. The first was a love story written specifically for my husband, John, and me. You can read and enjoy the story, but it is ours. However, the second love story is available to all. Will you allow God to woo and call you to Himself? Will you let Him capture you with His love? Will you accept His offer?

Love is a channel of God's blessing.

Something to Consider
1. When have you received unconditional love? When have you given unconditional love?
2. Tell how you have experienced the love of God.
3. How do you show others that you love them? How do you show God that you love Him?

Further Reflection
- Isaiah 61:10
- Zephaniah 3:17
- Romans 5:8
- 1 John 4:9–10

CHAPTER 6

WILL YOU MEET ME IN MY DREAMS?

Sometimes, John will wake me as he dreams; however, when the morning arrives, he rarely remembers his dreams. In contrast, I often remember my dreams. Many of them aren't important, like the dream of a never-ending bridge over the ocean. Some dreams are worrisome, like dreaming that I forgot to attend the one class that I needed to graduate. Some dreams I savor—vacationing in England with my husband and children, enjoying the beauty of the English countryside, and hiking through the Lake District. And frankly, some dreams are extremely funny, like the time I was an Irish dancer performing in our church foyer while my friend played the bagpipes. This dream got me moving so much that I woke up John. When he asked what I was doing, I sighed at his ridiculous inquiry; wasn't it obvious that I was in the middle of a very complicated Irish dance step?

Now, let me ask you a question. Have you ever invited God into your dreams? What about those nights when it takes a while to go to sleep or you keep waking up? During those times of wakefulness, it's helpful to pray or meditate on Scripture.

One such night, I extended an invitation to God. "Lord," I said, "would you please meet me in my dreams? You've given me some beautiful dreams over the years; would You meet me there more often?"

Before I tell you how God answered that prayer, let me share some of the ways that God has blessed me in my dreams. Five dreams stand out as treasured gifts.

======== 1 ========

"Have you seen Him?" they all asked.

I exited the grocery store, headed to my car with a load of groceries. A crowd gathered in the parking lot. Their voices were a mixture of excitement and wonder as they asked repeatedly, "Have you seen Him?"

Loading my groceries into the van, I listened to bits and pieces of their conversations. "He was here, right here in this parking lot! He spoke to me as if He knew me!" Filled with curiosity, I headed over to join the group of people.

A woman turned to me and asked, "Did you see Him, too?"

"Who?" I replied.

Everyone turned to look at me and spoke the same name at the same time: "Jesus!" My heart beat wildly at the thought that He'd been there. He was the One I'd talked to since early childhood, and if He was in the city, He must be found. I hoped an elderly man nearby had knowledge of where Jesus went. When asked, he wasn't sure, but he thought He might be headed to the hospital.

Trembling, I drove quickly, breaking the speed limits in my eagerness. There were no parking spaces open, so I pulled alongside the curb. In the hospital hallways, people ran about, laughing, crying, and shouting for joy. Many dressed in hospital gowns danced and leaped as if moving for the first time.

"He healed me!" they cried. "He touched me and healed me!"

Jesus had been there, but where was He now? I ran frantically from hallway to hallway, calling His name. Realizing He was gone, I began to cry. A man asked me what was wrong.

After listening to my long explanation, he smiled. "Jesus is headed to the airport. He has a flight to catch," he said. "If you hurry, you're sure to catch Him. Go quickly!"

At the airport, a crowd peered out the window at a plane getting ready to pull away from the gate.

"No!" I screamed in my head. "He can't be on that plane. I haven't seen Him yet!"

Maneuvering past the airport gate, I ran toward the moving plane with little thought of the security people running after me or the fact that I was behind an airplane getting ready to take off. I just had to see Jesus.

"Jesus, Jesus!" I cried. "Please don't go! I need you! Wait for me!"

No sooner had those words left my lips than the plane stopped. Gazing up at the plane, time stood still. The doorway opened, the stairs were let down, and there standing in the entrance was my Savior, my Lord—my precious Jesus! His face was hidden by the shadows, but I saw His hand reach down to me. God—reaching out to me! Taking several stairs at a time, I stretched out my hand to grasp His. Just as our fingers were about to touch, the dream ended.

This is one of my most cherished dreams. Upon waking, I could have screamed a thousand times over, "No! I don't want to wake up. Let me hold Your hand; let me see Your face." I often think about that dream, wondering what it would have felt like to have my hand enfolded in His. 1 Corinthians 13:12 says, "For now we see in a mirror dimly, but then face to face; now I know in part, but then I will know fully just as I also have been fully known." At the time, I only saw part of what God knew was going to happen many years later—that He would literally wrap my hand in His. But I'm getting ahead of myself. That's another story for a later chapter.

2

The calendar read *Elementary School Play*. The props were on stage in the cafeteria, where our weekly Girl Scout meetings took place. It was Christmastime, so it was appropriate that the play was about Jesus's birth. Children wandered around dressed as shepherds, wise men, and angels in white robes with white netted wings and golden halos. Dressed as an angel, I waited patiently to proclaim my greetings of joy to the audience, heralding the birth of Jesus.

As we moved to our places, there was something strange about the curtains hanging behind the manger scene. Shining from a tiny crack in the fabric was a very bright light. With ten minutes to go before the play began, curiosity took over. Looking around to make sure no one saw me, I snuck to the partially opened drapes. Stepping through, I closed the curtains behind me.

Suddenly, I wasn't on a stage. I was barefoot, standing on a dirt road leading down a hill. Night was falling, and a bright light shone on part of the town ahead. It looked like a star glowing more brilliantly than any had before. Walking toward the rustic buildings, I realized this was Bethlehem. A light that bright could only be shining down on the infant Jesus. I began to run, not minding the dirt and rocks in the road. Seeing Jesus became my main goal. Stopping momentarily to catch my breath, I closed my eyes and breathed in the cool air.

When I opened my eyes, I was no longer in Bethlehem, but in my bed. Pondering the dream's meaning, I thought of the words in Luke 2:11: "For today in the city of David there has been born for you a Savior, who is Christ the Lord." Another name for the Christ child is Emmanuel, "God with us." How awesome to think that Almighty God became a small child born in humble surroundings. God becoming man—there is a radical and wonderful truth.

3

So many sounds. If only I could have found a way to quiet them. I heard the shrill train whistle and the wheels clicking on the track. However, those sounds were overwhelmed by the cries of people locked in boxcars—hundreds of men, women, and children who were imprisoned for their faith in Jesus Christ.

Some of them called upon the name of the Lord, shouting to Him for strength and deliverance, knowing their deliverance meant martyrdom on His behalf. Others wept as they prayed, searching for His power and grace to carry them through this trial. Rising from the cacophony was the sweet sound of voices in song, singing praises to the One for whom they were willing to die.

My breathing accelerated as my husband and I crouched behind a large bush. Glancing across the pasture dotted with trees and bushes, John grabbed my hand and pulled me from the view of the train.

"Run with me. Now!" he urged.

It seemed we ran for hours, but where were we going?

A small building with a light shining through the window came into view. Approaching quietly, we saw the outline of a door in the dark. John knocked, not knowing who might answer. A small voice came through from the other side,

"Are you one of them?"

"What do you mean?" John asked.

"Are you Christians?" replied the voice.

There was only one way to answer, regardless of who was asking the question. Knowing that denying Jesus Christ was not an option, John boldly answered, "Yes, we are."

The door flung open, and a tall man asked us to follow. He led us to a rug-covered trap door that opened to a corridor under the building. Moving along the dark passageway, we heard singing in the distance. At last, a door was opened, revealing hundreds of Christians on their knees, their heads and arms stretched toward heaven. John and I joined this group of fellow believers. We were family, God's family. On our knees, with our heads and arms stretched upward with them, we joined in the chorus, "Every knee shall bow, every tongue confess that Jesus Christ is Lord!"

I awoke, confused. John and I were at a bed and breakfast with train tracks running nearby (a detail that was omitted from the B&B advertisement). Outside our window, a train rattled past, but in my ears, the chorus from my dream continued to resonate.

The words of Philippians 2:9–11 create a picture of the majesty and glory at the name of Jesus.

> *For this reason also, God highly exalted Him [Jesus], and bestowed on Him the name which is above every name, so that at the name of Jesus every knee should bow, of those who are in heaven and on earth and under the earth, and that every tongue will confess that Jesus Christ is Lord, to the glory of God the Father.*

What a glorious day that will be when we see the Lord and join the great chorus of praise to Him.

4

It was early morning; the curtains were drawn, but light made its way into my room. I sat up in bed and stretched. Walking to the window and pulling the curtains apart, I stood in wonder and amazement at the scene before me. Stretched as far as I could see were clouds that formed a series of individual pictures telling the story of the Bible. To all who looked up, God proclaimed His glory and the works of His mighty hand.

It started with the beginning of God's creation—a cloud-shaped picture of the earth with God's hand reaching down and forming it. Following that was Noah's ark, a dove, and a rainbow. The tablets that God gave Moses, the great temple in Jerusalem, a manger in Bethlehem, Jesus walking with His disciples, a cross with a crown of thorns, Jesus knocking on a door. It went on this way until the end, where a magnificent cloud with incredible beams of light shining forth from it caused me to believe that the return of Christ our King had come!

Surely others noticed this phenomenon. Heart racing, I ran back inside, found a telephone, and called my parents, my friends, and anyone else who would listen.

"Have you seen the clouds?" I asked. "Go outside and look at what God has done! He's making known to all mankind who He is and what He has done. Do you think Jesus is coming today?"

I hoped it was so. Even TV news reporters were marveling at the occurrence. Every channel had reporters talking about the wonder of the clouds and what they might mean.

I grabbed my car keys and headed to my parents' house. The house and yard were filled with people—mostly family, some unfamiliar, but all believing in Jesus and waiting for His return. Excitement ran through the crowd at the thought of seeing our King, and the words rang out, "He is coming! He is coming! He is coming!"

What did it mean? What do we learn from this dream? There's a wonderful set of verses in the New Testament that is very encouraging for believers.

> "Then they will see the Son of Man coming in a cloud with power and great glory. But when these things begin to take place, straighten up and lift up your heads, because your redemption is drawing near."
> —Luke 21:27–28

When it says to "straighten up and lift up your heads," that implies confidence. A confident person stands straight and holds his head up; a defeated person stands with shoulders slumped over and his head hung low. Thinking of the clouds in my dream with the light pouring from them, I stand confidently with my head held high, anticipating the return of Jesus, the King.

The Invitation
The Bible reminds us that God often spoke to people in visions or in dreams. There is a long list of people in Scripture who experienced God in that way—Abimelech, Jacob, Laban, Joseph, Pharaoh, Solomon, Nebuchadnezzar, Daniel, Pilate's wife, Paul, and John, among others. Even though several years have gone by with no dreams like those described, I continue to ask God to meet me in my dreams.

If I had my choice, He would talk to me every night in my dreams as well as in the daytime, but that isn't so. When He feels the time is right, He'll meet me in my dreams again, where I'll be waiting.

You may wonder if God answered my specific request when I invited Him into my dreams. Here is the answer.

One evening, my father called to tell us about a suspicious-looking spot on one of his kidneys; he was scheduled for a series of diagnostic tests to determine if it was cancerous. Both Mom and Dad have always experienced good health, so the situation was new, scary, and troubling. What if something bad happened to my daddy?

That night, I dreamed that I was speaking at my father's funeral. Waking up startled, I prayed for God to remove the spot on Dad's kidney. Dozing off to sleep, I was troubled by another dream. This time, I was singing at my father's funeral. Upon waking, the tears flowed freely.

"God," I prayed, "I know my daddy loves Jesus and that when he dies, he will be with You. That is a very good thing. But, honestly, I'm not ready for him to die. I love him so much. Please take care of him and let him be okay. Don't let me return to those troubling dreams. Meet me in my dreams, Lord, that my mind would be at rest and think about something other than a funeral."

Time passed. Eventually, sleep came.

5

I was standing alone in the dark. Beams of light shone through the cracks of the only door in the room.

Leigh Ann!

I looked around, but couldn't see anyone. The voice, however, was familiar. "Yes Lord," I replied, "I am here."

Leigh Ann, do you see that door in front of you?

"Yes Lord, I do."

I want you to step forward and open it. Then walk through the door and enjoy yourself.

What did He mean? "What will I find there, Lord?"

I could hear the smile in His voice as He spoke. *Leigh Ann, just open the door, enter, and enjoy your time.*

I stepped forward and grabbed the doorknob. On the other side of the door in my grandmother's kitchen were my mother, Aunt Nancy, and my grandmother. They were clearing the table, washing dishes, and laughing about something. My grandmother's presence was perplexing because she had passed away many years before.

"Lord, what's happening? How is MaMa Kee here?"

God gently encouraged me again to enjoy my time. MaMa walked toward me with a huge smile on her face. She hugged and welcomed me, inviting me to join them in the kitchen.

MaMa's kitchen was a treasured place where I had spent many hours as a child. She told me to grab a plate and get some lunch. The wonderful smell of her cooking filled the room, especially the pie sitting on the countertop that she made just for me. Her chocolate pie with whipped cream was always a favorite.

The food was delicious, the conversation delightful, and the time too short. Sensing that it was time to go, I hugged MaMa closely.

She smiled in her sweet way and put her hands on my face. "Darling, it's time for you to go."

"But MaMa," I said, "it's been so long since we've been together. I love you so much and miss you terribly."

She assured me that she was extremely happy with her new home in heaven and that she would indeed see me again one day soon.

I woke feeling an incredible peace and comfort. Never had a dream seemed so realistic. I could smell, taste, touch, see, and hear all things as if experiencing it firsthand. My heart overflowed with gratitude to God for His presence in my dream.

He also heard my prayers regarding my father. The spot never disappeared, but it was not a great concern for the doctors. The real answer to my prayer, however, was not that my father was healed. It was the hope and confidence I gained that regardless of whether Dad was healed or not, God cared for him.

This life is not the end.

My father has since passed away. God's strength, grace, and comfort carried me through his death and allowed me to do the very thing I never thought I could do. At Dad's celebration of life service, I spoke about my father and the role he played in shaping my life. Before and after the service, I played some of his favorite hymns on the piano.

My heart is full of hope, knowing Dad is in the presence of Christ, more alive today than ever before.

I've often wondered about the meaning of these dreams. Some Christians spend a great deal of time studying and trying to understand dreams and visions. They would likely have an explanation for my dreams. I simply see someone who desperately wants to be with Jesus. I think about Jesus often during the day, so much that it doesn't surprise me that this carries over into my dreams.

Do you seek Jesus; do you hunger and thirst for Him? Jesus promises in John 6:35, "I am the bread of life; he who comes to Me will not hunger, and he who believes in Me will never thirst." When we diligently seek Him, we will find Him!

Nothing happens in life that escapes God's attention or knowledge. He knows every little thing about our lives, and He cares deeply about each of those things. Why? Because He loves us!

How about you? Let me ask you once again—have you invited God into your dreams? He may meet you there. But even if He doesn't, that's okay.

We should talk to God and ask Him to work in our life; we should seek His face, be still, and listen for Him. How God responds might be different for each of us, but He promises to answer in His own perfect timing.

When you lie down tonight to sleep, extend the invitation for God to draw close to you, whether in your waking hours or in your sleep.

Sweet dreams!

Dreams are a channel of God's blessing.

Something to Consider
1. Do you remember your dreams?
2. What do you seek? What do you think about? What do you treasure?
3. Will you invite God into your dreams? Why or why not?

Further Reflection
- Psalm 4:3–4
- Psalm 121:1–8
- Proverbs 3:24
- James 4:8

CHAPTER 7
THE UNSEEN HANDS

It was a day of great privilege and honor. Mrs. Wesson, my second grade teacher, asked me to run an errand for her.

"Leigh Ann," she said, "would you please take these papers and deliver them to Mr. Howie, the principal?"

As I walked to the teacher's desk, I puffed my chest out and held my head a little higher. Special papers in hand, the click of my shoes on the square floor tiles echoed down the long empty hallway. Once at the school office, I announced to the secretary that I had something for the principal. That was big stuff for a seven-year-old.

Let's take this idea to a grander scale, when God calls you to do something for Him or to carry out one of His instructions. That happened to me in 1993.

I'd been married for three years, and we were living in Texas. While I walked with the Lord most of my life, I was still a relatively young Christian. John and I were active in our church and had made many friends. One of them, Melissa, shared some details about her life that made me realize how different our upbringings were.[14] While I grew up with a very rich spiritual heritage focused on Jesus Christ, her spiritual heritage was one in which Satan was very active. Because of that, Melissa was a target for all kinds of supernatural activity.

Thankfully, Melissa chose not to follow in the steps of her family, but rather to follow Jesus Christ. Because of that decision, Satan made her life a living hell. Many nights in the fall of 1993, a group of her closest friends and a local pastor gathered round her to cover her in prayer. The women invited me to participate, but recognizing my immature faith, I decided not to go. Instead, I joined them in prayer from the safety of my home. This went on for weeks.

When December came, John and I headed to his parents' for the Christmas holidays, our usual tradition. A few days before Christmas, John and I went to bed. Because we were in John's childhood room, we were sleeping in twin beds on opposite sides of the room.

At three a.m., I was awakened by someone gently shaking me; someone's hands were literally holding onto my arms. I sat up expecting to see John standing by my side, but he was sound asleep across the room. There was no one by my bed.

You need to pray for Melissa, a voice whispered.

I shook it off, thinking I was dreaming, and settled back onto my pillow. As I dozed off again, the same hands shook me, more firmly this time.

I bolted upright, my heart racing.

You really need to pray for Melissa, the voice repeated.

I shot up a quick prayer asking God to be with Melissa and stretched out again when a set of unseen hands held me by my arms. The voice came again, persistent and direct.

You need to pray for Melissa, right now!

I did what I was told. The remainder of the night I sat up in bed, praying for Melissa like I'd never prayed before. I prayed God would protect and deliver her from trouble. I prayed that if I could take any part of Melissa's burdens from her, God was welcome to place them upon me.

As the sun rose, I fell asleep, exhausted.

When I woke up, pain shot through my neck and shoulders. I told John what happened during the night and about my discomfort. He suggested I call Anne, who often prayed over Melissa in the middle of the night. When she answered the phone, I shared my experiences from the previous night and told her about my pain.

"Is Melissa okay?" I asked.

Anne was silent for a few moments on the other end of the line. Finally, she replied that around 3 a.m., there was a group praying over Melissa. They cried out to God to awaken His saints to join them in prayer. As for my pain, Melissa's arms had been dislocated from their sockets in the night; a doctor who was present put them back into place.

Then, we were silent. God woke me up! He gave me Melissa's pains! Who am I that the God of all creation would wake me up to pray for someone else? Who am I that He sees me as worthy to bear another's pain? How humbling that God sees me as someone who is important. He loves me! He loves you, too, and wants to use you in ways that you cannot imagine.

It's amazing to learn that God allows supernatural events through the actions of simple, everyday people. Ephesians 2:10 reminds us that "we are His workmanship, created in Christ Jesus for good works, which God prepared beforehand, that we would walk in them." God knew before the beginning of time that He would have me pray for my friend Melissa.

When we pray, whether we see things happen or not, we can be assured that God hears our prayers. How do we know that? He says so in His Word.

Psalm 91:15 is one of many verses in which God assures us that He hears us when we call on Him. God says, "He will call upon Me, and I will answer him…." That is why we should never give up hope in praying for something or for someone.

My friend, Melissa, was well acquainted with the enemy.

She explained that when believers pray, it's like pouring burning gasoline on the enemy—that's how much he hates it.

Be encouraged by 1 John 4, in which John tells us to test the spirits and that any spirit that does not confess Jesus is not from God. Verse 4 reads, "greater is He who is in you than he who is in the world." Or, as I think about it: *Greater is the One and Only True God who is in you than Satan who is in the world. What hope and power those words hold.*

The story does not end here though. Following Christmas Day, John and I traveled to my parents' house in North Texas. As I replayed all that happened the previous week, a new conviction settled in. I needed to write Melissa a letter and mail it to her that same day.

Prior to our Christmas travels, I started studying the spiritual gifts. I wanted to discover my gifts and how to use them to God's glory. Little did I know that He was about to reveal one—the gift of encouragement. Writing to Melissa and recounting all that happened, I told her exactly what I'd been praying for her. Here is a small excerpt of that letter.

> I want you to know that I am praying for you throughout the day and each time I wake up at night, as well. I ask the Lord to strengthen you, to heal your heart and mind. In my thoughts, I can see Jesus with His mighty arms wrapped around you, giving you comfort and protection and assuring that all will be well.

I was seeking a verse in Scripture to share with her, but was not sure where to look. Opening my Bible to John, two verses grabbed my attention. I sensed that same voice telling me to write those verses down to encourage my friend, reminding her that He hears prayer. I ended the letter with these words:

"So I close this letter thanking the Lord as Jesus did in John 11:41–42: 'Father, I thank You that You have heard Me. I knew that You always hear Me...."

Evidently, she was encouraged by the words that the Holy Spirit gave me to write, for she read my letter to the church when she shared her testimony many months later. Today, she continues to follow Jesus Christ. Her life hasn't been easy, but she knows the source of her strength.

Has God been asking you to do something, some act of service? How have you responded? The Bible says in Colossians 3:23–24, "Whatever you do, do your work heartily, as for the Lord rather than for men, knowing that from the Lord you will receive the reward of the inheritance. It is the Lord Christ whom you serve."

Did you catch that last sentence in verse 24? You were created to serve God. When you pray for people and follow through with action, you are doing just that (see Matthew 25:35–45).

Upon waking every morning, founder and former president of Campus Crusade for Christ International, Bill Bright, would pray, "Lord, think with my mind, love with my heart, speak with my lips, wear me as a suit of clothes."[15] It is my desire to do whatever it is that God wants me to do. I just want to serve Him. What about you?

The supernatural is a channel of God's blessing.

Something to Consider
1. Is God asking you to do something—some act of service? What is your response?
2. Why do people often discount the supernatural?
3. How many verses in the Bible can you find that speak of God being able to accomplish the impossible?

Further Reflection
- 2 Corinthians 10:3–4
- Ephesians 6:10–13
- Colossians 4:2
- 1 John 4:4

CHAPTER 8

I AM NOT MY OWN

While driving home late one night, I hit a low point. God wanted to talk; I did not. So, I turned up my radio as loud as I could to drown Him out (not a good idea!).

After several minutes, the Holy Spirit spoke to me. *You can turn up your radio as loud as you like, but I'm still here. I'll still be here whenever you turn it off.*

One way or another, God and I were going to deal with the problem.

So what is this grand struggle in my life? A powerful nine-lettered word—*surrender*. To surrender is "to give oneself up or to yield to the power of another." As a follower of Jesus Christ, we yield or surrender to Him as our Lord and King, not because He wants to overpower or dominate us, but because He, the Creator, wants a relationship with us, His creation. He desires for us to know Him, to trust that He has all things under control. We don't just entrust certain things like our circumstances, our finances, or our emotions to Him. We're called to surrender everything, all of it—spouse, children, friends, possessions, health, schedules, even our own lives.

Surrender is woven throughout this book and the different seasons of my life—asking with a child's faith for Jesus to be my Lord and Savior, crying out to God for relief from panic attacks, and allowing God to choose my future spouse. One would think this would get easier, but it doesn't.

Through my conversations with various people, it's apparent that this is a common daily struggle. Some godly role models I look up to admit to having a difficult time with surrender. While I'm sorry that so many have a hard time with this, I'm encouraged that I'm not alone. It is my prayer that you, too, will be encouraged as you read about my own journey and the discoveries I've made along the way.

A Defining Moment
From September 1995 to April 1996, while living in Bryan, Texas, I experienced an epiphany—a clear lesson and a marked attitude regarding surrender. During those seven stressful months, our apartment lease ended on April 15, John became unemployed in May, he began applying for history positions at universities far from family and friends in Texas, I was a new mother who had quit my teaching job to stay at home, and all three of us—John, David, and I—were sick. We weren't a little stressed out. We were overloaded with stress.

In the midst of that, the first four of those months were met with incredible silence from God. That was new for me. I've heard it called the "dark night of the soul" or "a desert experience." Right when things were falling apart and I needed God the most, it seemed He had abandoned me.

September through December, I prayed for direction for our lives, searching the Scriptures for a word of hope. By the time January arrived, I was at my wits' end.

On a cold, dreary day, John took our infant son to the mall. Both felt quite ill, but they were tired of being closed up in the apartment. My headache from that morning had turned into a full-blown migraine, and I laid alone in the darkness. I was hurt and angry with God for His silence.

I pulled the covers over my head. "Just what if I choose not to believe in You anymore?" I screamed at God. "What are You going to do about that?"

Hearing those words from my mouth, I froze. A choice had to be made—I could either choose to believe and trust Him or abandon the God I loved. Accept or reject? I immediately recanted my challenge, asked for forgiveness, and began crying. I made my choice. Regardless of the circumstances, I couldn't let go of Jesus, and I'll always trust Him, even when He's silent. That was a defining moment for me.

You probably know the Bible story of Shadrach, Meshach, and Abednego. These three refused to worship the idol that Nebuchadnezzar had set up. As a consequence of disobeying the king's command, they would be thrown into the fiery furnace. Their response to the king's threat is amazing.

> *"If it be so, our God whom we serve is able to deliver us from the furnace of blazing fire; and He will deliver us out of your hand, O king. But even if He does not, let it be known to you, O king, that we are not going to serve your gods or worship the golden image that you have set up."*
> —Daniel 3:17–18

God could save me from my circumstances that seemed to spin out of control, but even if He didn't, I would still trust Him. Through the experience of these three courageous men, I realized that God is with me at all times, even when He is silent.

Philip Yancey writes about this. "God has not promised a state of constant bliss or a problem-free existence but has promised to be present in the silence and in the dark, to exist alongside us, within us, and for us."[16] Even more encouraging is God's assurance to us in Hebrews 13:5, "I will never desert you, nor will I ever forsake you."

During those four months of silence, God didn't abandon me; He was still there. When life appears to be falling apart, we cannot rely on our feelings or on the way things seem to be. Our emotions and situations are undependable and unpredictable. We must turn to God's promises in His Word that are always dependable and never change.

On January 10, 1996, just one week after my epiphany, I asked God to give me something from Scripture to hang onto and give me hope. After letting my Bible fall open, I looked down to read for the first time Jeremiah 29:11–14.

"I know the plans that I have for you," declares the Lord, "plans for welfare and not for calamity, to give you a future and a hope. Then you will call upon Me and come and pray to Me, and I will listen to you. You will seek Me and find Me when you search for Me with all your heart. I will be found by you," declares the Lord.

Now I had Scripture to accompany my defining moment and a budding new attitude that changed my life and gave me confidence that God would always be by my side.

Our apartment lease ended on April 15. However, two days earlier, John got a job as an assistant history professor at Quincy University. We stayed at my in-laws' house for several months before moving into our new home in Illinois. With some questions answered, our stress level went down and our health began to improve. God provided for all of our needs, and His presence was constant, even in our season of great change.

All To Jesus I Surrender
One of my favorite memories growing up is sitting in "big

church" between my parents.[17] A hymn we often sang was "I Surrender All."

Recently, while attending my sister's church in Texas over Christmas vacation, the pastor closed the service with this song. Tears came to my eyes as I thought of my struggle with surrendering to God. As the pastor finished his final prayer and I stood to sing the beloved hymn, the pastor paused.

"Someone here today has been seriously thinking about the words to this song and the meaning of surrender," he said.

I laughed out loud and thought of raising my hand and saying, "Yes, that would be me, sir."

Let's look at the words written by Judson W. Van DeVenter in 1896.

"I Surrender All"
All to Jesus I surrender; All to Him I freely give;
I will ever love and trust Him; In His presence daily live.
All to Jesus I surrender; Humbly at His feet I bow,
Worldly pleasures all forsaken; Take me, Jesus, take me now.

All to Jesus I surrender; Make me, Savior, wholly Thine;
Let me feel thy Holy Spirit; truly know that Thou art mine.
All to Jesus I surrender; Lord I give myself to Thee;
Fill me with Thy love and power; Let Thy blessing fall on me.

All to Jesus I surrender; Now I feel the sacred flame.
O the joy of full salvation! Glory, glory, to His Name![18]

Although there are many lessons to learn from this hymn, let's consider three truths that are applicable to our lives. These truths, while written carefully to express one man's personal journey with surrender, are scriptural truths. The ideas seem quite simple, but if we daily put these into practice, our relationship with Christ will grow all the more intimate and tender.

Lesson 1: Living Daily in the Presence of Jesus
Several years ago, I came across a pair of Bible verses that struck me as essential for a godly outlook and attitude. Acts 17:25 alludes to the awesomeness of God because of what He has done: "He Himself gives to all people life and breath and all things." This thought continues a few verses later in Acts 17:28, when Paul writes, "For in Him we live and move and exist...."

We have our being by living in Him—not just beside Him or near Him or next to Him, and not by hearing about Him, but by living in Him. If we live, move, and exist "in God," it stands to reason that we had better be seeking and living in His presence daily.

How do we do this? By inviting Jesus Christ into our everyday lives before our feet hit the floor and we get out of bed. "The will of God for your life is simply that you submit yourself to Him each day," says Kay Arthur. She continues by praying, "Father, Your will for today is mine. Your pleasure for today is mine. Your work for today is mine. I trust You to be God. You lead me today and I will follow."[19]

As we go through our day, we look for ways God is working and moving; we listen and tune our ears that we might be sensitive to hearing His voice; we talk to God about our joys, trials, struggles, and relationships; and we read His Word. When we fail, we pick ourselves up and start again, being reminded that "The Lord's lovingkindnesses indeed never cease, for His compassions never fail. They are new every morning; Great is Your faithfulness" (Lamentations 3:22–23).

Lesson 2: Realizing That We Belong to God
This is something that I have known for a long time with my

head, but my recent struggle with surrender allowed this concept to burrow deep into my heart. When I stopped running and began talking with God about why surrender was so difficult, it came down to realizing that I belong to God. Don't get me wrong—I love that I'm His child and that I belong to Him. That's not the part I get hung up on. It's the other part that troubles me. If I belong to God, that means I am not my own. If I am not my own, I can't do things my way. So it all comes down to the sins of pride and selfishness.

I can relinquish many things to God, but one that gets me every time is giving up my will for His, whether that's my time, my plans, or my worries. And it hurts to write that. Though the truth hurts the most, that is also where renewal begins and God's grace and mercies are extended to us. I will always eventually surrender to my Lord because I made that choice in Bryan, Texas, on that dark day in my bedroom. Not surrendering isn't an option for me. The problem lies in how quickly I surrender. Will it be several weeks or several years? Too often it seems the latter.

The apostle Paul is a kindred spirit when he writes of his own personal struggles. "For what I am doing, I do not understand; for I am not practicing what I would like to do, but I am doing the very thing I hate" (Romans 7:15).

As God and I have worked on this problem area in my life, He has reminded me over and over that I belong to Him and that I am not my own. For the past several weeks, every time I sit down to read my Bible, He has revealed to me other verses that talk about that very thing (these are listed in Appendix B).

One passage stands out in particular—1 Corinthians 6:19–20. It refers to our body being a temple of the Holy Spirit and reminds us that we are not our own; we were bought with a price. What is that price? The horrific death of Jesus Christ on the cross for our sins. May we never forget that we belong to God and are not our own. We live to do His will, not our own.

Lesson 3: Experiencing the Fullness of His Love, Power, and Blessing

Experiencing the great abundance of God's love, power, and spiritual blessing is what the apostle Paul prayed for his friends at the church at Ephesus. These words are special, as they have become my prayer, not only for myself, but for everyone who reads this book.

> *For this reason, I bow my knees before the Father, from whom every family in heaven and on earth derives its name, that He would grant you, according to the riches of His glory, to be strengthened with power through His Spirit in the inner man, so that Christ may dwell in your hearts through faith; and that you, being rooted and grounded in love, may be able to comprehend with all the saints what is the breadth and length and height and depth, and to know the love of Christ which surpasses knowledge, that you may be filled up to all the fullness of God.*
> —*Ephesians 3:14–19*

"Blessed be the God and Father of our Lord Jesus Christ, who has blessed us with every spiritual blessing in the heavenly places in Christ" (Ephesians 1:3). Praise God, from whom all blessing flow! Every. Spiritual. Blessing. There's an inexhaustible fullness of God's love, power, and blessing, which the prayers of His children can never use up. Whatever we think or ask, God can do exceedingly and abundantly more. And when we believe that He's outdone Himself, He can go beyond that. The full extent of His love for us surpasses our knowledge; it's incomprehensible. We'll never fully grasp His love on this side of heaven. Yet Paul prays that believers will be filled with the fullness of God. As we spend time daily in intimate fellowship with our Lord, realizing we are not our own, we will experience a relationship with Him beyond what we could imagine.

Restoration
After running from God to avoid the stark reality of my sin, I've surrendered. Let me tell you why I took off my running shoes.

Over the Christmas holidays while spending time with family in Texas, God poured out blessing after blessing upon me. After being so disobedient, I felt unworthy of the good things He sent my direction.

In the middle of the night, I laid in bed and talked to God. Why would He continue to bless me when my behavior didn't warrant anything good? I contemplated the words of Psalm 139:7–10 and could relate to David's words.

> *Where can I go from Your Spirit?*
> *Or where can I flee from Your presence?*
> *If I ascend to heaven, You are there;*
> *If I make my bed in Sheol, behold, You are there.*
> *If I take the wings of the dawn,*
> *If I dwell in the remotest part of the sea,*
> *Even there Your hand will lead me,*
> *And Your right hand will lay hold of me.*

I confessed my sin before God and told Him I was tired of running.

In the silence of the room, the Holy Spirit spoke to my spirit. *You can run, Leigh Ann, but I will chase you, because you are Mine!*

I don't understand that kind of amazing love, but I do desire, believe, accept, and invite it into my life. All the time my Lord had been chasing me. The image of His holy arms wrapped tight around me brought unexplainable peace that night. Along with His peace came another unexpected surprise—the words that I've just written for this chapter. At four a.m. in the darkened living room of my parents' house, I penned the thoughts that came to me from the Lord.

It's my desire that the transparency of this chapter will offer hope and encouragement to readers who find themselves in similar circumstances. To some extent, we all have areas that are difficult to relinquish to God's control. So often, we surrender to the Lord, but then turn right around and reel it back in.

Elisabeth Elliot wrote, "If my life is surrendered to God, all is well. Let me not grab it back, as though it were in peril in His hand but would be safer in mine!"[20] There is great freedom in letting go of the things that entangle us and allowing Him to take over entirely. God offers a trade—His life for ours. The price was extremely high on God's end: Jesus voluntarily endured the cross for you and me, our sin for His death. But look at what He offers us in return—His free gift of eternal life in Christ Jesus our Lord (see Romans 6: 23). I can think of no greater exchange than that.

Surrender is a channel of God's blessing.

Something to Consider
1. Why do we feel the need to control our lives?
2. Fill in the blank: God, I will give you anything but _____. Why is that area so difficult for you to surrender to Him?
3. What changes do you desire God to work in you so you can surrender to Him willingly and joyfully?

Further Reflection
- Isaiah 43:1
- Acts 17:24–28
- 1 Corinthians 6:19–20
- Ephesians 3:17–19

CHAPTER 9

AWARENESS OF THE HOLY SPIRIT

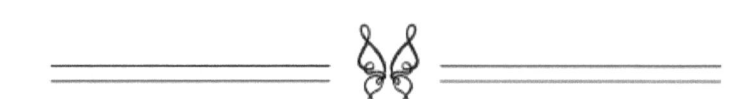

Our love for Christ is revealed in our obeying His commands. Christ has set the example of love and obedience, and we are expected to follow. To help us do this, Scripture says that we are given the gift of the Holy Spirit, God living within us.

In John 14:15–17, Jesus tells His disciples,

"If you love Me, you will keep My commandments. I will ask the Father, and He will give you another Helper, that He may be with you forever; that is the Spirit of truth, whom the world cannot receive, because it does not see Him or know Him, but you know Him because He abides with you and will be in you."

We may not always feel the Helper's presence; however, the Bible is clear that He is there.

The Holy Spirit does many things in the lives of believers.
- He is our Helper.
- He convicts us of sin.
- He guides us into all truth.

- He illuminates Scripture, bringing understanding.
- He reveals the deep things of God.
- He teaches.
- He prays for us when we are not able.
- He comforts us in our grief.
- He helps us tell others about Jesus.
- He strengthens.
- He encourages.
- He helps us become more like Jesus.

Since giving my life to Jesus Christ, it's been a daily process of learning to be sensitive to the Holy Spirit—listening to Him; learning from Him; and accepting His guidance, encouragement, and instruction. I wasn't good at this as a child. Even now, I am still learning. During my first year of marriage, I experienced the power of the Holy Spirit—power that He directed toward me.

On three different occasions over the course of twelve years, I encountered the power of the Holy Spirit. Each one reveals how God accomplishes His purposes.

1

"When they [Philip and the eunuch] came up out of the water, the Spirit of the Lord snatched Philip away; and the eunuch no longer saw him, but went on his way rejoicing. But Philip found himself at Azotus. . . . "

—Acts 8:39–40

In 1990, I was teaching elementary music in the Texas public school system. Being the music teacher for the entire school gave me the opportunity to interact with rich, poor, black, white, and Hispanic students. They came with a variety of life experiences ranging from loving homes with church youth groups, dance classes, and family vacations to dysfunctional families filled with physical and drug abuse, jailed parents, gangs, and Satanism.

The latter were such a problem that the local police department's crime prevention unit held a daylong workshop on this topic at our church. I knew the information would make me uncomfortable. However, it allowed me to understand what some students were encountering. I needed to be there.

Upon entering our church, I looked for a familiar face. Except for a few staff members setting up, I was on my own. I took a packet of information from a police officer and sat at a table with two people—a woman across from me and a man at the far end of the table. The woman's dress and makeup were colorful, as was her abundant red hair. She said hello to me with a heavy foreign accent.

After the police officer began his lecture, I was troubled at the creepy material. He explained a series of symbols, markings, hand signs, and drawings with specific meaning to those who worshiped the enemy of my God.

See the lady across from you? Why don't you ask her if you can pray for her?

I looked around, but no one was looking my way. My heart pounded. I was scaring myself silly. I was focused on the police officer when I heard it again.

The lady across from you—ask if you can pray for her.

The Holy Spirit was speaking to me.

"Are you kidding me?" I prayed in response. "I don't know this woman, I've never met her before, and You want me to ask if I can pray for her? She'll think I'm nuts!"

For the next hour, this exchange went back and forth between the Holy Spirit and me. I'd never had a conversation like this with God before. Several minutes would go by, and then the prompting question would come again, each time worded a bit differently.

Are you going to go ask her? It will be okay. Ask her!

I doggedly argued my point. As a result, I don't recall anything taught that day regarding Satanism in our schools, but I'll never forget the Holy Spirit speaking to me. It's a wonder that God was so patient, for I was anything but obedient.

As the meeting wrapped up, the red-haired woman went to the other side of the room. God prompted me to walk over and ask if I could pray for her.

In my stubbornness, I crossed my arms, sat down, and thought, "No! I won't."

A torrent of questions ran through my mind. "What would she think of me? What if I couldn't answer her question? What if everybody in the room was watching me?"

The adrenaline pumped through my body. What happened next, I cannot explain; I just know it happened. One moment, I was sitting at the table with my legs and arms crossed refusing to do what God had clearly asked me to do. The next moment I was standing directly in front of this woman.

Some 2,000 years earlier, in the eighth chapter of Acts, Philip heard the Holy Spirit tell him to witness to an Egyptian eunuch outside of Jerusalem. At the end of the story, Philip baptized the eunuch. As soon as they came out of the water, the Holy Spirit snatched Philip away. One moment Philip was standing before the eunuch, and the next moment he was miraculously transported more than thirty miles away to the seacoast town of Azotus.

Like Philip, God moved me from one place to another. There I was, in front of a stranger, my mouth hanging open.

In her accented voice she said, "Excuse me, may I help you?"

I looked at her. Clearing the lump in my throat, I said, "Actually, ma'am, I believe that I'm supposed to help you. You don't know me, or I you, but I was wondering if I could pray for you."

Tears began flowing down the woman's face, causing her

makeup to run. She explained that she'd been praying for God to bring someone to pray for her son.

When God asked me to speak to her, I should have listened the first time. I felt truly humbled that He was willing to work with me and use me in spite of my failure to obey.

The woman and I went to another room where she shared her story. She grew up in Romania in a gypsy family. Her grandfather was a medium, her mother a fortuneteller, and other family members had psychic abilities. The woman told me that her only son was currently in prison in the United States. She knew it was his just punishment, but she was deeply concerned for him. He was hearing voices and being tormented by some unseen evil in his cell.

Going on, she said that she believed in the power of prayer. Then she asked me to pray for her incarcerated, tormented son, Franklin. I told her that I, too, believed in the power of prayer, that Jesus Christ has overcome the enemy in this world.

I never saw the woman again. To this day, whenever God brings Franklin to my mind, I pray he's delivered from what tormented him and has found refuge in Jesus Christ.

I'm so thankful that the Holy Spirit didn't give up on me. If He had, I would've missed seeing this woman's prayer answered and God work supernaturally in my life.

2

"But when they hand you over, do not worry about how or what you are to say; for it will be given you in that hour what you are to say. For it is not you who speak, but it is the Spirit of your Father who speaks in you."
—Matthew 10:19–20

In January 2000, I first led a women's Bible study, the Interdenominational Women's Bible Study in Quincy, Illinois.

We were studying one of my favorite books of the Bible, the gospel of John. I'd studied John previously and was looking forward to going through it again to glean new insights from God.

Excited and nervous, I felt a weight of responsibility in teaching the Bible and presenting God's Word in an accurate and truthful way. My limitations in this area were many. I lacked confidence in my ability to lead, clearly answer questions, quote and find verses from Scripture, and teach a group of strangers. Relying fully on God to equip me to lead would only be accomplished through His strength, not mine.

Each week, I prayed, "Lord, decrease me. I ask that You would increase in me. Please use my mouth to speak what You'd have me to say." I wanted the Holy Spirit to use me as His instrument, working through me to speak to these women.

That particular semester, there was a woman who was curious about what the Bible taught. She often said things that were not scripturally accurate. She believed that missing a church service was a sin, worshiping God had to take place in a church building, and she'd grow wings and become God's angel after she died.

One week, we had a large group in our class, and this lady was there. I started praying in my typical fashion, asking the Holy Spirit to take over as I led. Midway through the lesson, we came to a passage of Scripture that sparked a lively discussion. She looked puzzled. I tried several different explanations of what the Bible was saying, but this lady just didn't get it.

In my frustration, I silently cried out to God, "Help me! She doesn't understand, and I don't know how to say it any other way." I needed to calm down and try it again in a different way.

I faced her once more and started talking. Or rather, the Holy Spirit spoke through me. It was almost as if I was sitting on the side of the room watching what was happening. Explaining the passage of Scripture to her, I heard myself quoting several Bible verses from memory.

"I didn't know that I knew those verses from memory. How did I know that? I don't!" I thought to myself.

As I spoke, her eyes lit up. She said, "I get it! Now I understand." Then, she explained it back to me clearly.

I marvel over the way God works. That day, His Spirit took over and did something that on my own I couldn't do. He brought clarity and understanding to a confused situation.

Remember what Matthew 10:19-20 tells us. "But when they hand you over, do not worry about how or what you are to say; for it will be given you in that hour what you are to say. For it is not you who speak, but it is the Spirit of your Father who speaks in you." While Jesus is speaking to his disciples about persecution because of their belief in Jesus Christ, these verses are equally relevant to all who call on His name. In my case, I was clearly not in a place of persecution, but was in a place of need, to present His Word in such a way that brought understanding and clarity to one who was seeking Him. When God gives a promise in Scripture, He keeps that promise. If He says He is going to do something, then He'll do it. We must take Him at His Word and trust that He'll help us in our time of need.

3

So they went into the ark to Noah, by twos of all flesh in which was the breath of life. Those that entered, male and female of all flesh, entered as God had commanded him; and the Lord closed it [the door] behind him.
—*Genesis 7:15-16*

Have you ever faced a persistent question? From January to March 2001, three unrelated women, on three separate occasions, asked me the same question: "Do you know of any Bible study offered in our town that explains how the Bible is put together, what the different books teach, and what the major themes are?"

I didn't know these women and am not sure how they got my name. It grieved me to say there wasn't a Bible study like that in our town.

One afternoon in the first week of March 2001, my phone rang. A woman asked me the same question again. We talked for a bit about the type of study she wanted to join. It saddened me to again say there was no such offering, but I took her name and number just in case.

As I set the phone down, I heard a voice. *Why don't you do it?*

I knew that voice. It was the Holy Spirit speaking clearly to my inner being.

He asked again, *Why don't you do it?*

I thought of all the reasons why I shouldn't start a new Bible study: I didn't have time or know the material. Beyond the four women who called me, I wasn't sure who would come to that type of study. The reasons why I couldn't do it rolled through my mind.

With my hand still on the receiver and my mind seeking a way out, the phone rang. It was my friend Joyce.

"What are you doing right now?" she asked.

I laughed and told her I was arguing with God (not something I suggest anyone do). She didn't think that was funny and wanted to know what I was struggling with. Irritated, I rehashed the details of the previous months. I told her about the Holy Spirit's question and attempted to justify why I couldn't start a Bible study. Or if I did start one, why it would have to be later in the year.

"Leigh Ann," Joyce said, "why would you wait until the fall to do God's work, when there is a need right now? You need to offer this study now."

That was not what I wanted to hear, but I listened. Joyce is a woman of the Lord whom I trust for wise counsel. She was right, whether I wanted to admit it or not.

That night, I prayed about what God wanted me to do, knowing that He'd already made His plan clear. Sitting on our shelves was *30 Days to Understanding the Bible in 15 Minutes a Day!*, a book written by Austin, Texas, pastor Max Anders.[21] I was familiar with the author, having heard him preach on several occasions at Grace Covenant Church. In the book, Anders explains the Bible's structure, content, and major themes, the very topics these women wanted to learn about.

John and I talked and decided to do the study in our home once a week on Tuesdays. We wanted to create an environment that was intimate, nonintimidating, and accessible for people from different denominations.

The next hurdle was determining whom to invite. Only God knew who needed to be there. In the movie *Field of Dreams*, Kevin Costner's character, Ray, is a farmer from Iowa who receives an interesting message about building a baseball diamond in the middle of his cornfields: "If you build it, he will come."

Ray built a field and miraculously, Shoeless Joe Jackson and seven other Chicago White Sox players from 1919 appeared on the field. In the last scene of the movie, a long line of cars drives toward the baseball field.

I had a similar sense regarding this Bible study. When praying about it, I sensed God saying, *If you offer the Bible study, I will bring the people.*

We made information fliers and distributed them around town. The fliers read,

Do you desire a basic knowledge of the Bible?
Would you like to learn how the Old and New Testa-

ments relate to each other?
Then come join us in a new Bible Study, "Understanding the Bible."

As women called inquiring about the class, they wanted to bring their husbands as well. Uncomfortable with the thought of teaching men, I asked John to pray about leading the class with me. I have a great deal of respect for my husband's ability to teach Scripture; as a history professor, he has a special gift in explaining the historical context of when things happened in the Bible and how. After praying about it (and I must confess, some serious begging on my end), John agreed to join me in this new adventure God offered.

On Tuesday, March 20, 2001, John and I set up our family room for the first class. Out the window, a line of cars parked in front of our house, and fifteen people came that night. I knew a few of the women, but the majority I'd never met. John knew no one.

We were amazed at what God was doing. Like the story in Genesis, in which God brought animals to Noah two by two, male and female, God brought the people He had chosen to our home to study His Word. What would have been impossible for Noah to carry out, God took care of. What seemed like an impossible task for us, God had well in hand. In faith, we extended the invitation, and in faith, we welcomed each person into our lives. God took care of the rest.

Over the course of the next five years, John and I opened our home on Tuesdays during the fall, winter, and spring. We studied Nehemiah, Mark, 1 & 2 Timothy, Revelation, and the spiritual disciplines. While each class differed in attendance, thirty-seven people came to study God's Word, many staying for several classes, some staying for all. God blessed us with the perspectives of many denominations: Catholic, Church of Christ, Apostolic, Methodist, Lutheran, Presbyterian,

Non-Denominational, and Baptist.

John and I watched the class makeup change over the years; each time God provided exactly the people who were supposed to be there. That first year, the majority of people attending had never studied the Bible before. So we focused the first couple of years on grounding people in God's Word.

As time went by, the focus changed. By then, many class members were well versed in Scripture and had a good working knowledge of the Bible. This made for enlightening discussions. The last year, we spent a year studying the book of Revelation. Once again, the class was filled with those who knew God's Word well. By the end of that year, John and I knew that we were moving to Tennessee. Our work in Quincy was finished; it was time to follow a new calling.

Looking back, we stand in awe of God's marvelous plan— the people we met with that last year have stepped out and are leading in the ways God has guided them. One directs a Bible study in his parish, a couple started a Bible study in their home, three other couples started a new church that has grown exponentially, and others have taken leadership roles in local ministries.

Reflecting over the years, I marvel at how the Holy Spirit works. He accomplishes the miraculous, fills mouths with His words, does the impossible, equips His followers for service, and carries out His perfect plan. Watching Him work in my life and the lives of others, I am increasingly confident in surrendering to my Lord. When He asks me to do something out of my comfort zone, it's getting easier to say, "Yes, Lord!" because I know He will enable me to do whatever He asks.

What is the Lord asking you to do? How will you respond? Trust Him and take that step of faith. You may find yourself standing in complete awe at the wonderful and surprising ways that God works in your life.

The Holy Spirit is a channel of God's blessing.

Something to Consider
1. Do you have the Holy Spirit living in you? Do you recognize Him when He speaks to you?
2. How has God moved you outside your comfort zone? Are you willing to remain there?
3. How have you experienced the power of the Holy Spirit? What is your story?

Further Reflection
- John 14:16–17, 26
- John 16:13–15
- Romans 8:11
- 1 Corinthians 2:10–13

CHAPTER 10

THE FINGERPRINTS OF GOD

It was Halloween. Five-year-old Rachel, dressed as a Renaissance princess, was eager to walk around the neighborhood and fill her bag with candy. John agreed to walk with her in hopes of lifting her spirits from the disappointment of our church canceling its fall festival due to inclement weather.

As John and Rachel headed down the street, I washed dishes from dinner and offered up a brief prayer. "God, please reign on this day."

Outside, the sky turned pink, gray, and gold. Framed in the front window, a large, vibrant rainbow stretched across the sky for all to see. Above that rainbow was a second, equally stunning, complete rainbow. And above the second were the pale colors of a third rainbow!

It was as if God was crying out through the triple rainbows, *I AM!*

In my wonder and uncontained excitement, I began to speak aloud, "That's right! He reigns! My God reigns on Halloween!"

I ran to my neighbor's house, knocking until the pastor and his wife came to the door.

"You have to see this," I told them. "You will appreciate how God is making Himself known."

What a God we serve! Now, every October 31 serves as a reminder of the day that God showed Himself through His creation of the rainbow.

Nature Is God's Classroom
For much of my life, I ran from one activity to another, immersed in an overloaded schedule, rarely stopping to appreciate the subtle reminders that God is all around me. Somewhere in the midst of this frantic pace, something changed. Witnessing the wonder and pleasure my small children took in seeing nature slowed me down to experience things from their perspective. This presented many teachable moments.

I'd take my children on what we called "praise walks." During these, we'd look for different ways to praise God through His creation. The beautiful colors in the sky during a sunrise or sunset showed God to be an artist, full of creativity and with a pallet of every imaginable color at His disposal. We loved watching the clouds and making pictures out of them, but our favorites were those illuminated by God's light and color. Just like when Jesus ascended into the clouds (Acts 1:9), we were reminded of His long-awaited return (Acts 1:11).

Walking into our backyard was like settling into God's classroom with rich lessons waiting to be learned. Watching a long string of ants carrying food to their home opened up the opportunity to talk to my children about the wisdom of the ant. Ants prepare their food in the summer and then gather during the harvest (Proverbs 6:6–8), and God created us to work as diligently as these ants.

One autumn day, the children found a baby bird that left its nest too soon and was vulnerable in the open yard. While finding a makeshift shelter for this fledgling, we talked about how God remembers the birds and provides their food every day (Luke 12:24). If He cares for the birds, He will certainly care for us. We are so much more valuable to Him!

The backyard was not our only outdoor classroom. While exploring our family's land in Texas, we usually ended up by the creek. Seeing a towering cottonwood planted by a stream of water was the perfect opportunity to tell David and Rachel about a tree in the Bible. Psalm 1:2–3 says that the one who delights and thinks about the word of God will be like a tree firmly planted by streams of water, yielding fruit—not withering, but prospering.

Many lessons were learned through the weather that blew in with the different seasons.

Spring thunderstorms were opportunities to speak of God's amazing power. When David was two years old, a large storm left a full rainbow in the sky. I whisked David onto my shoulders, ran out the back door into the light rain, and showed him that our God was the keeper of promises, that the rainbow is God's way of remembering the promise He made and reminding every living creature that never again would a flood destroy all men as in the days of Noah (Genesis 9:11–17).

Living in Illinois, winter always brought snow. It was not a matter of *if* the snow would come, but *how much*. Sitting in front of our big window, the children and I watched huge snowflakes fall gently and quietly. We talked about Jesus and how He forgives us of our sins. Isaiah 1:18 says, "Though your sins are as scarlet, they will be as white as snow...." Nature reminds us of that which is both profound and certain.

Nature + Scripture = Revelation
Walking with my children and observing nature allowed me to acknowledge God's handiwork, talk about it, and thank and/or praise Him for it. As in the school classroom where you open a textbook to glean more information on a subject, you must open the Bible to really learn about God and this world that

He made for us.

Do you realize how often God speaks about His creation? Reading about birds, animals, flowers, rainbows, trees, mountains, water, thunder, wind, the sun, and the soil impressed upon me that these are important to Him. In Scripture, each one is used in parables, analogies, and metaphors as object lessons on how to live as God intended, as descriptors of God's attributes, and as reminders that He, who loves us so much, is closer to us than we realize. The fingerprints of God are everywhere, waiting to be discovered.

Growing up in north Texas and then living near the Midwest cornfields, mountains were only viewed through pictures or on the occasional vacation. Now, living in eastern Tennessee, I view the mountains every day and never fail to appreciate their amazing sight, for they were established by God's strength (Psalm 65:5-6). Driving over the ridge, I remember the encouraging and hope-filled words of Psalm 121:1-2: "I will lift up my eyes to the mountains; from where shall my help come? My help comes from the Lord, who made heaven and earth."

What about the stars? "Lift up your eyes on high and see who has created these stars, the One who leads forth their host by number, He calls them all by name; because of the greatness of His might and the strength of His power" (Isaiah 40:26). If God cares so much about the stars that He knows them by name, how much more does He care for you—the one He created to have an intimate relationship with?

Can you relate to the words of Psalm 63:1? "O God, You are my God; I shall seek You earnestly; My soul thirsts for You, my flesh yearns for You, In a dry and weary land where there is no water." There is another reference to nature: the desert. Are you longing for something, or are you wandering through some kind of desert in life that causes you to be dry and weary?

Be encouraged and don't lose hope, for God's provision

and blessing never run dry. He creates fountains of water in that dry, weary land. He brings new life into impossible situations. When the Israelites were wandering in the desert, thirsty and exhausted, God came through.

> *"The afflicted and needy are seeking water, but there is none,*
> *And their tongue is parched with thirst;*
> *I, the Lord, will answer them Myself,*
> *As the God of Israel I will not forsake them.*
> *I will open rivers on the bare heights*
> *And springs in the midst of the valleys;*
> *I will make the wilderness a pool of water*
> *And the dry land fountains of water."*
> —Isaiah 41:17–18

God knows our needs. He also knows our deeper needs and offers us His water. This is not the water found in an ocean, river, well, or stream. Jesus offers Himself, the Living Water. In John 4:13–14, Jesus speaks not just to the woman at the well, but to all who read His words.

> *"Everyone who drinks of this [well] water will thirst again; but whoever drinks of the water that I will give him shall never thirst; but the water that I will give him will become in him a well of water springing up to eternal life."*

Next time you're outside, take a deep breath. Then take another. Breathe in the air and let it fill your lungs. As you do so, think about God's breath that sustains you, holds you together, and keeps you from turning to dust—that is humbling. Job understood this sobering thought. "If He should determine to do so, If He should gather to Himself His spirit and His breath, All flesh would perish together, and man would return to dust" (Job 34: 14–15).

Thanks be to God for His sustenance! We see that Jesus Himself gives to all life and breath. It is in Jesus that we live and move and exist (Acts 17:25–28). God created the earth in such a way that we can see Him and know Him; His creation reminds us of Him and His Son. We are without excuse, for He is all around us. We need to open our eyes—notice and believe.

Lessons from a Garden
Upon moving to our new home, John and I worked to transform a weed-infested backyard into a tiered garden adorned with an arbor, trellis, and fence. During an early spring, the plants were in full bloom, making for a lovely garden.

Having lunch on our screened-in back porch with a new acquaintance, I commented on how beautiful the flowers were, to which our guest said, "Ah, where your heart is, your treasure lies."

I was taken aback and saddened by the comment because this person had no idea why I gardened. I didn't desire to compete with my neighbors. Had I been thinking more clearly, I would've explained my initial interest in gardening came from enjoying my mother-in-law's pretty flowers. Her comprehensive knowledge of plants, the elegant design of her flowerbeds, and her understanding of color inspired me to try my hand at it. Gardening gives me pleasure.

One such pleasure is the sweet fragrance of a flower. Fresh cut peonies or French lavender arranged in a vase smell like perfume. As believers in Jesus Christ, we are to be a sweet aroma whose fragrance others cannot help but notice. When I look at my flowers, I see people, for many of the flowers were gifted to me from people I love. There are Daddy's dwarf irises, Anabelle's rose, Sandy's day lilies, Mr. John's peonies, Robin's irises, and Mama Kee's amaryllis, which she originally got from her mother and my great grandmother! The roses were purchased with "seed money" by the group of women I taught in Illinois. The plants remind me to pray for those who gave them.

I also have frequent visitors to my garden—butterflies. An extraordinary number of butterflies, especially yellow ones, enjoy my flowers and my company. I often wonder if God sends the butterflies my way because He knows I notice and enjoy them. Every time a yellow butterfly flutters by, whether in my garden or somewhere else, I immediately think of God and take a moment to talk with Him. Childlike joy and wonder spring up, amazement that God takes a caterpillar and transforms it into a butterfly. It's such a beautiful reminder of how He transforms His children through the work of the Holy Spirit to reflect His Son.

Flowers aren't the only things growing in my garden. I also have a full range of culinary herbs. Cooking with fresh herbs reminds me of God's creativity. This is seen in the beauty of a rosemary bush, the vibrant color of chive flowers, and the peculiar shape of a dill plant. When rubbing the leaves between your fingers, smell the wonderful fragrance of lemon thyme. Experience the incredible burst of flavor of freshly chopped, sweet basil sprinkled over tomatoes. God's creation is filled with amazing variety that He created to appeal to all of our senses.

I loved working with the soil, tending the flowers and herbs, and keeping the weeds and pests in check. But I also felt close to God in my garden. He filled my thoughts and talked to me about life. Pruning and weeding the garden became reflections of things that needed daily removal in life. Control issues? Pluck that one out. Sarcastic words meant to irritate? Cut. Ignoring a need? Snip away. Being selfish? Clip.

Battling aphids, rose slugs, and Japanese beetles paralleled the disastrous effects of habitual sin. When left alone, these pests tear through a rose bush, leaving it stripped of its leaves and displaying deformed and discolored buds. How similar to my life when I allow sin to run amok. I become anxious, stressed, critical, unkind, and disagreeable.

I also learned the importance of observation. Plants tell it like it is. Wilting flowers need water, blackened leaves usually mean fungus, yellowing leaves that wither and fall off suggest overwatering, and leaves with holes indicate pests.

Sometimes we can read people like we can plants. The art of observation is more than simply seeing a person. It is intentionally paying attention to those around you. Notice body language, tone of voice, and facial expressions. When we pray to see people as Jesus does, our eyes are opened to see beyond the surface. A slight grimace or slumping shoulders clue you in that despite what may be said initially, something is going on below the surface. When it comes to relationships and people, exercising spiritual discernment with God's grace can take you from superficial to deeply meaningful.

Sometimes all it takes to go beyond the surface is a smile, a genuine question, and a willingness to listen.

Stop and Smell the Roses (or at Least Slow Down)
God has revealed what He is like in creation. His eternal power and divine nature—His invisible attributes, are made visible through nature (Romans 1:20). What else can we learn about Him by looking at the natural world? God is perfect, awesome, incomparable, multifaceted, splendid, majestic, intelligent, creative, and powerful. He is the God of order, beauty, and intricate details.

In Scripture, God tells us to consider, behold, meditate, muse on, and praise Him for His handiwork. Each command requires action. To do these, we must stop to appreciate the splendor of what is around us. Stop. At a minimum, we must slow down.

Train your senses to be aware of nature's beauty. Notice the leaves falling from trees, breathe in flowers' fragrance; or listen to birds singing outside your window. You never know how God might reveal himself unexpectedly through such a humble act.

Nature is a channel of God's blessing.

Something to Consider
1. What can you do to slow down in order to appreciate the beauty around you in the natural world?
2. Discover something to appreciate in God's creation every day, even if it is one thing. Smell a flower, watch a thunderstorm roll in, listen to the sound of running water, or study the clouds.
3. When have you experienced the presence of God in nature?

Further Reflection
- Psalm 89:11
- Psalm 95:3–5
- Isaiah 61:11
- Romans 1:20

CHAPTER 11

THE EASTER EGG

Do you believe in miracles? Have you ever found yourself in one of these scenarios?

You discovered a parking space at the front of the grocery store.

That conference you hoped to attend was sold out for months. Miraculously, at the last minute, a ticket became available.

You asked your children to clean their rooms, and they answered happily, "Okay, anything to help out."

These could all be called miracles. (The last one may be an actual miracle.) The word *miracle* is often tossed around without much thought to the magnitude of a real, honest-to-goodness miracle from God.

During the 2003 Easter holiday, I experienced a miracle that stopped me in my tracks and made me refocus my attention on the true meaning of Easter.

While attending a Bible study leaders' meeting to prepare for the next week's lesson, we opened with a time of prayer. I prayed that during the upcoming Easter weekend, God would keep me from losing sight of why we celebrate Easter. Life at that time was busy with David's upcoming birthday celebration and our family Easter traditions. When asking God to slow me down for time to meditate on what Christ did for me, I asked as a doubting Thomas.

"Just how, exactly, are You going to get my attention?" I asked God. I didn't have to wait long for the answer.

Saturday afternoon before Easter, my family dyed eggs. I let the kids dye my share of eggs, though they persuaded me to decorate one. In previous years, I carefully planned my eggs' designs. This year, however, there were too many things that needed to be done. A simple design would have to suffice.

Using a blue permanent marker, I hurriedly drew a large cross on one side of the egg. On the opposite side I wrote, "He Is Risen," and drew sunrays surrounding it. The egg was colored orange, left to dry, and placed back into the carton.

Later that day, three-year-old Rachel wanted to look at the eggs. Sitting on the floor by the refrigerator, we opened the carton.

Rachel held up my egg. "Mommy," she said, "who is that on the cross?"

There, centered on the cross, was the form of Jesus Christ, His arms reaching out to me. God had my attention. Having talked about Jesus Christ many times, I reminded Rachel of what He did on the cross for every person—He loved us so much that He died for us.

I called John. Thinking there was an emergency, he ran downstairs to the kitchen. Holding up the egg, I asked what he saw.

John, having seen me hurriedly decorate my egg earlier that day, turned it over in his hands. "Whoa!" he said. "There's something you don't see every day. That looks like Christ on a cross."

What a special gift from God—being forced to slow down in the midst of a whirlwind weekend to have my thoughts consumed by His message: *I love you!*

1 John 3:16 captures this idea. "We know love by this, that He laid down His life for us. . . ." This little egg became an extension of God's grace that motivated me to move beyond the cares of this world and truly focus on my Lord.

That evening after checking the egg a dozen times or more, I noticed that the image of Christ was beginning to fade. What was left was a small heart centered on the cross. When I called my parents to share this extraordinary experience, my father inquired if the image would be there in the morning. Thinking about Easter Sunday, we agreed that He would no longer be on the cross.

Here was the ultimate teachable moment for David and Rachel: Jesus Christ died and came back to life. What a message of hope!

Before going to bed, the kids and I made Easter story cookies. (Recipe can be found in the back of this book in Appendix A.) Through the preparation and cooking of these simple meringue cookies, we talked about the arrest, crucifixion, death, and resurrection of Jesus Christ. The addition of each ingredient symbolized something significant that took place during that first Easter weekend.

When beating the egg whites, we talked about how white represents purity, that we can be pure by having our sins cleansed and washed away by Jesus. Another lesson arose when each child "sealed" the oven "tomb" with pieces of tape. They felt sad to leave the cookies in the oven overnight, just as Jesus's followers despaired when His tomb was sealed. Heading off to bed, David and Rachel were reminded of the hope that awaited them that next morning.

Easter morning, the children and I rushed downstairs to check on my miracle egg. Christ had faded from the cross. After marveling at the empty cross on the egg, we opened the oven "tomb" to check on our cookies. Each meringue was cracked and hollow inside, another reminder of the risen Christ and the empty tomb.

God answered my prayer in a powerful way, and our family still reminisces about that unforgettable Easter weekend every spring. To keep God's love foremost in my mind, photographs of the egg are tucked in my Bible.

What miracles have you experienced in your life? You may not have an Easter egg story, but you've probably experienced something that could be called miraculous. Sometimes you can hold a miracle in the palm of your hand; other times, all you have to do is look around. When was the last time you held a newborn baby? God knit that child together in their mother's womb. A baby is a miracle.

Look outside your window and view the trees. Notice how each tree is different. Man can plant the seed for that tree; however, God causes it to grow and determines its size, shape, color, and texture. That is a miracle.

Have you sat in an airport or shopping mall for any length of time? People watching is fascinating. Each person is unique in their own way. Much like those trees, every person has a distinct shape, size, color, and personality. Every human being is God's workmanship (Ephesians 2:10). Whether they believe in Him or not, He created them. Not only did God create you, He knows every detail of your life intimately. That is a miracle.

Here is one more example to get you thinking. Next time you're outside at night and away from the city lights, stop and behold the stars in the sky. On our family's land in Texas, I love lying in the bed of the pick-up truck and watching the stars. Because there are no city lights, the heavens are clearly visible. Some stars burn brighter than others, while the planets radiate light. In this setting, the hazy band of the Milky Way galaxy takes shape. What an amazing sight and miracle from God.

Considering the magnitude of God's creation, I think of the words in Psalm 8:3–5.

When I consider Your heavens, the work of Your fingers,
The moon and the stars, which You have ordained;
What is man that You take thought of him,
And the son of man that you care for him?
Yet you have made him a little lower than God,
And You crown him with glory and majesty!

Take a moment to slow down and appreciate the miracles that surround you every day. It's hard to notice them when you're running from one place to another. You must purposefully look for God's miracles around you. Do this regularly, and you'll develop the habit of being aware of God. Ask Him to help you recognize His handiwork. Then take the time to thank Him for it. He works in remarkable ways and in simplistic ways. We just need to look for Him.

Miracles are a channel of God's blessing.

Something to Consider
1. Do you believe that God still works miracles, signs, and wonders today? Why or why not?
2. Big miracles always make a lasting impression. Name some miracles that you see in everyday life that are sometimes easy to overlook.
3. What miraculous thing has God done in your life lately?

Further Reflection
- Exodus 15:11
- Psalm 77:14
- Daniel 4:2–3
- Acts 15:12

CHAPTER 12

LESSONS IN SUFFERING

Sorrow, grief, anxiety, heartache, pain, tribulation, misery, anguish, hurt, trial, and affliction—if you had to sum up all of these in one word, what would it be? What synonym would you choose?

Now consider what people in these situations have in common.

- Grieving the unexpected death of a son.
- Facing consequences with the law because of poor choices and emotional issues.
- Enduring persecution in the workplace for believing in Jesus Christ.
- Watching an elderly mother die.
- Struggling with the emotional scars of an abusive past.
- Losing a daughter and husband within a month of each other.
- Receiving a diagnosis of terminal cancer.
- Experiencing months of excruciating physical pain.

This time, the words from the first list become real-life experiences. Do you see their common link? They're all suffering.

Each example relates to real people I've prayed for or ministered to during their time of suffering. Before writing off the idea that blessing can come from suffering, stop. Please don't skip ahead. This chapter is full of God's blessing and hope for those who are suffering or helping others who are hurting.

From the best of my knowledge, nobody on the list above purposefully invited suffering into their life, except one—me (experiencing excruciating physical pain). I know, I know, why would I invite such a thing into their life? Was I really in my right mind? I had no concept of what I was asking God, or of the lessons that would follow in the next several years. God instructed me in the School of Suffering and showered me with some of the greatest blessings I've ever experienced.

Learning about Grief
In the summer of 2003, I searched my shelves for books to read during my upcoming vacation. Richard Foster's *Prayer: Finding the Heart's True Home* was one of them. I'd tried reading it on two other occasions, but only made it through a few pages.

In the book, Foster examines various forms of prayer, from simple prayer to unceasing prayer and everything in between. As I began reading the chapter called "The Prayer of Suffering," I realized that up to that point in my life, I'd never really suffered. Sure, difficult things had happened before, but suffer?

At the end of the chapter was a prayer to which I related, so I sincerely prayed:

> O Holy Spirit of God, so many hurt today. Help me to stand with them in their suffering. I do not really know how to do this. My temptation is to offer some quick prayer and send them off rather than endure with them the desolation of suffering. Show me the pathway into their pain. In the name and for the sake of Jesus, Amen.[22]

I finished reading Foster's book as Wednesday morning Bible study was starting up in September. Little did I know the women in my group that year would be instrumental in teaching me about suffering.

It all started with Mary, who was new to my small group. Every week she came to Bible study downcast, looking like she'd been crying. One Wednesday, she shared that her son had died unexpectedly the previous year. Her grief was unlike anything I'd seen, as if a heavy load weighed down her entire being. As I sat with her, she sobbed.

Not knowing what to do, I prayed, "God, how do I help this woman? I don't know what to do."

Immediately, the answer came. *Mourn with her and share in her burden.* Romans 12:15 tells us to mourn with those who mourn, and Galatians 6:2 says to bear one another's burdens. As I took these verses to heart, I wrapped my arms around Mary and wept with her.

Henri J.M. Nouwen was quoted in our study guide that year.

> Those who can sit in silence with their fellowman, not knowing what to say but knowing that they should be there, can bring new life in a dying heart. Those who are not afraid to hold a hand in gratitude, to shed tears in grief, and to let a sigh of distress arise straight from the heart can break through paralyzing boundaries and witness the birth of a new fellowship, the fellowship of the broken.[23]

I was beginning to understand Nouwen. Not only did God handpick our group of ladies that year, but He'd also chosen our study guide on Ruth and Esther as well. Many of the lessons addressed trials and grief, giving helpful advice and

Scriptures to those hurting. One lesson gave specific suggestions on how to comfort the mourning.

It was beautiful to see those suggestions played out as our group rallied around Mary and ministered to her through meals, letters, phone calls, prayers, shared tears, and hugs.

Early that next spring, one of my voice students was working on a solo for church—Crystal Lewis's "Beauty for Ashes." I was struck by the lyrics, which were fitting for Mary's life.

> When sorrow seems to surround you,
> When suffering hangs heavy o'er your head,
> Know that tomorrow brings
> Wholeness and healing.
> God knows your need,
> Just believe what He said.
> He gives beauty for ashes,
> Strength for fear,
> Gladness for mourning,
> Peace for despair.[24]

Mary had faith in Jesus Christ. Despite her circumstances, she knew God loved her. We talked about Psalm 56:8, which brought her great comfort. "You have taken account of my wanderings; Put my tears in Your bottle. Are they not in Your book?" Mary commented that she knew God understood her pain, because He, too, lost His Son.

From September 2003 to April 2004, God took a broken woman and brought healing to her heart. At the close of our study, I kept in contact with Mary in order to encourage her. She was ready to get on with life and went back to work as a nurse helping others. Three months later, Mary died unexpectedly in her home. Now, grief was at my door.

It was an honor to give the eulogy and sing "Beauty for Ashes" at Mary's funeral. Her life was no longer weighed down by fear, mourning, despair, sorrow, and suffering. In the presence of Jesus Christ, beauty, strength, gladness, peace, wholeness, and healing were her new permanent companions.

God's blessings to me that year were of a different flavor, as they were lessons about how to minister to the grieving. Lessons learned included:

1. The world is full of hurting people who suffer for a number of reasons, whether it be death, illness, persecution, divorce, physical pain, unforgiveness, or sin. Don't assume you've figured out everybody who comes your way.

2. When ministering to those who are grieving, be willing to share in their sorrows. Sit, listen, cry, laugh, and be silent with them. So often, words aren't needed.

3. Encourage the hurting person, but be careful not to be preachy or churchy with them. The Holy Spirit is excellent in the area of comfort as He is the Great Comforter; He'll give you discernment when it is appropriate to share Scripture.

4. Through the experience of grieving with others, God equips you to help those hurting souls that He'll bring your way in the future.

5. God is amazing! He beautifully plans and coordinates everything perfectly. In my case, putting the right group of people together, using the study guide that the leaders had chosen, and answering prayers all showed God's care. Nothing is coincidental. All things are providential.

Following that year, I assumed I was finished with suffering and could move on to happier spiritual lessons. But now it was time to learn about suffering firsthand.

Learning from Physical Pain
In November 2004, I began experiencing terrible chest pains. A visit to my doctor and several diagnostic tests showed an inflamed gallbladder that needed to be removed. Since the pain

was sporadic, the surgeon cleared me for travel to Texas for Christmas and scheduled surgery a few weeks later upon my return.

This trip was supposed to be a fun visit with family and friends, but turned into a medical nightmare. Several days after arriving at my in-laws, I was heading to the emergency room with crushing pain in my chest. I'd never felt pain like that before, not even in childbirth. Riding in the backseat with John and my father-in-law, Bob, in the front seat, I grabbed my Bible for words of comfort. It fell open on Psalm 34:1. "I will bless the Lord at all times; His praise shall continually be in my mouth."

"Okay," I thought. "I can do this; I will bless my Lord while in extreme pain."

However, the pain was so severe that it impaired my thinking; crying and moaning, I looked for another verse. I found Psalm 34:8: "O taste and see that the Lord is good; How blessed is the man who takes refuge in Him!" I begged God to let me take refuge in Him and be released from the pain. Turning the pages for another verse, Psalm 91:15 stood out. "He will call upon Me, and I will answer him; I will be with him in trouble. . . . " I wasn't guaranteed the pain would go away, but Scripture assured me that God was my refuge, He was very aware of my situation, and He was there with me.

Sobbing, I waited five long hours in the emergency room. John and Bob, equally frustrated by the lack of medical care or concern from the emergency room staff, tried to console me. A chaplain saw my distress and prayed for me. Discouraged and tired of waiting, we were finally introduced to the doctor, who after a series of tests determined what we already knew—my gallbladder was inflamed and full of gallstones.

After I was moved to a hospital room, Bob left to help my mother-in-law care for David and Rachel. Exhausted, I fell asleep, only to be awakened by a sound that I rarely heard, the sound of my husband crying. John, who usually demonstrates great strength in difficult situations, was broken by frustration and worry. We talked, prayed, and telephoned friends in Quincy, Illinois, which made us both feel better.

I was scheduled for surgery to remove my gallbladder, a routine procedure that took three hours due to complications. After I recovered, the doctor released me to spend Christmas with my in-laws.

On Christmas Day, we headed to Plano to see my family. Within a few hours of greeting my parents, the terrible pain returned, only this time, it was worse. While waiting for an ambulance, I asked John if I was dying.

"Absolutely not!" he responded.

Surrounded by paramedics and traveling to yet another hospital, it dawned on me to pray for myself. During my first hospital stay, my prayers centered on my worried husband and my in-laws who were caring for our children.

With an oxygen mask on, needles in my arm and hand, and not a care in the world as to what the paramedics thought, I cried out repeatedly, "Jesus!"

At the emergency room, I was evaluated, given pain medication, and released. When the pain returned, I was back in the hospital again the next day. Somehow, fifteen gallstones were missed during my previous surgery, and another procedure was required to remove them.

John and I despaired. We were away from our home, distant from our friends, in unfamiliar hospitals with unfamiliar doctors, missing holiday gatherings with family, watching the bills accumulate, and once again waiting for a doctor. Feeling helpless, desperate, and abandoned, we telephoned friends in Quincy and begged for prayer.

Within hours, our friends gathered in the sanctuary of our home church. These people came from the different ministries that John and I were involved with—from church, Cursillo,

Walk to Emmaus, Bible studies, and prayer groups.[25] One of our close friends later gave his perspective of what went on in Quincy at this gathering.

> An unusual aspect of this prayer group was that many had never met each other, but the body of Christ was clearly evident in the diversity of Christian backgrounds and church affiliations (including Catholic, Methodist, Presbyterian, Non-Denominational, etc . . .). These two dozen friends and fellow believers came together literally at the foot of the huge cross that hangs so prominently in the sanctuary of First Presbyterian Church.
>
> This gathering provided a powerful demonstration of God's power and fulfillment of Scripture in James 5:15-16, where "the prayer of faith will save the sick person . . ." and also to "pray for one another, that you may be healed." With hands and hearts joined together, prayers were voiced requesting God to provide healing and proper treatment for Leigh Ann, favor and guidance, encouragement, peace, and much more. God's grace, guidance, and love were evidenced in a mighty way through this event.[26]

The power of prayer is truly remarkable. One friend prayed I would have an advocate. That's when my doctor appeared, scheduled my procedure, and set things in motion. Another friend prayed for me to experience the presence of God. Her prayer ushered in one of the most amazing blessings I've ever experienced.

As the nurses prepared me for the procedure, I was frightened. The doctor offered words of encouragement. While praying, I drifted into unconsciousness. Upon waking, I was on my back with my eyes closed and could feel someone holding my right hand, stroking and patting it. Enveloped by a great peace,

I wondered who was comforting me. I opened my eyes to find no one there, but someone was there, for I felt a hand on mine.

"Lord," I quietly asked, "who holds my hand?"

I was immediately aware that Jesus Christ held my hand. Although He couldn't be seen, I could physically feel His presence. He patted my hand one last time and let it go; I began to cry, for I didn't want Him to leave. The nurse, alerted by my crying, smiled as I told her what had happened. She told me Jesus was her Savior too.

I'd like to say that was it: lessons learned, body healed, back home in Quincy, all good to go. But that wasn't the case. From January through March 2005, I endured the same excruciating pain, another emergency room visit, two hospital stays, and two more procedures to remove the remaining gallstones. However, those three months were filled with an abundance of blessings.

- The outpouring of love and prayer from all of my brothers and sisters in Christ in Quincy and scattered all over the United States.
- Church members gathering around me to lay hands on, pray, and anoint me with oil.
- The sweet prayer of my friend and pastor as he stood by my hospital bed.
- Having my best friend in the emergency room and the laughter we shared as the drugs took away my pain and impaired my ability to speak and think coherently.
- The opportunity to tell my hospital roommate and her husband about Jesus Christ and His incredible peace.
- Waking up in the middle of the night in a quiet room, thinking I was alone, only to see another close friend sitting beside me reading her Bible, and the humility of having her assist me to the bathroom with all the medical equipment hooked onto me.
- The regular meals brought into our home, as well as

flowers, cards, visits, and phone calls. One card, sent from Saint Peter's Catholic Church, was signed by 179 parishioners who were praying for me, most whom I didn't know.

- Having my friends who worked in the medical field make sure I received the best possible care while in the hospital.
- Having special friends arrive early in the morning to help get David and Rachel ready for school and then drive them there.

Rereading the cards and letters received during that time, I'm blessed all over again. The outpouring of love from our friends is something that will always be cherished.

"Lord, What Can We Learn from Our Circumstances?"
During my four hospital stays, I never asked God why this was happening to me.

Instead, I asked, "Lord, what do You want me to learn from this experience?"

Suffering comes in many forms: emotional, spiritual, financial, mental, relational, and physical. Maybe you're hurting right now and are seeking answers. Thinking about the mysteries of pain and suffering, I often come away with as many questions as answers. However, when I inquired from God what He wanted me to learn from these difficult experiences, He taught me some things that may be of help to you.

When we suffer, hope is always there, and hope has a name—Jesus Christ. We aren't guaranteed that our suffering will be removed. We're promised that Jesus will be by our side, that He'll never leave us or forsake us (Deuteronomy 31:6, 8 and Hebrews 13:5). Jesus Himself knows about suffering. We're not alone; He's able to sympathize with us in our weakness, as it says in Hebrews 4:15–16, but if we keep reading, we're told to "draw near with confidence to the throne of grace, so that we may receive mercy and find grace to help in time of need." Jesus is our hope.

God also uses suffering to reveal Himself to us in ways He otherwise might not.[27] I believe God reveals Himself however and whenever He wants, but in our sufferings, when we cry out to Him, He lavishes His grace on us in an extra special way.

I learned firsthand about God's peace that surpasses all understanding. It was an incredible blessing to experience the tangible and unseen presence of my Lord. Shortly after that experience, God spoke to me through His Word. "'For I am the Lord, your God, who takes hold of your right hand and says to you, Do not fear; I will help you'" (Isaiah 41:13, NIV). In *Reaching for the Invisible God*, Philip Yancey wrote, "A relationship with God does not promise supernatural deliverance from hardship, but rather a supernatural use of it."[28]

Whether we see it or not, God causes all things to work together for the good of those who love Him.[29] He brings great good out of dark times. Foster's words encourage us.

> But here is the wonder: the suffering is not for nothing! God takes it and uses it for something beautiful, something far beyond anything we can imagine. Right now we catch only glimpses here and there, the moon's reflected light. But a day is coming when the blinders will be removed and the scales will fall off, and then we will see a glory in our sufferings that will blaze like the noonday sun.[30]

Sometimes we need to let go of our expectations of how we think things should happen. While in the hospital, John and I mourned the loss of family dinners, long walks, and the warmth of conversation around the fireplace. We had plans and were devastated when they fell apart. We'd forgotten, but came to remember, that we're to live each moment trusting in Jesus, relying fully on Him. This is often difficult to do. We get scared when things are out of control and try to take over and figure it out on our own. That's why we're to take refuge in God, who is always in control.

When we find ourselves in difficult circumstances, we need to let friends and the Christian community minister to us. It's okay to allow the body of Christ to take care of you. In my opinion, it's much easier to give than to receive. During my third hospitalization, it was important to graciously accept the help coming our way. When we don't let people help us, we deprive them of the blessing that comes in serving others.

I have no regrets in asking God to teach me about suffering. Through an innocent prayer, God taught me volumes about life.

Where are you right now? Is life moving along smoothly? If so, draw closer to Jesus, so when trials come your way, you have a strong foundation to stand on. Are you low in the valley right now, up to your neck in heartache? Then be encouraged and full of hope, for Jesus is close by.

When alone and hurting, I sing "All Who are Thirsty." Sometimes the words are sung with passion, and other times the words barely leave my lips.

> All who are thirsty,
> All who are weak,
> Come to the fountain.
> Dip your heart in the stream of life.
> Let the pain and the sorrow be washed away
> In the waves of His mercy
> As deep cries out to deep.
> Come, Lord Jesus, come.

Come, Lord Jesus, come.
Holy Spirit, come.[31]

Wherever you are in life, seek the One who brings hope. Come, Lord Jesus, come.

Suffering is a channel of God's blessing.

Something to Consider
1. What has God taught you during your season of suffering? If you are there right now, ask God what He wants you to learn from your circumstances.
2. How have you distanced yourself from another person's sufferings? Why?
3. Name some positive things you've experienced through trials. What blessings or joys came your way?

Further Reflection
- Romans 5:3–5
- Romans 12:15
- Galatians 6:2
- Hebrews 4:15–16

CHAPTER 13

THE BLESSING OF A GIFT

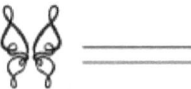

It's fun to receive a gift. Gifts often come on a birthday or at Christmas, but there's something extra special about a present that comes out of the blue. I received two gifts at God-appointed times. One opened up my season of personal suffering, while the second came the week after my fourth hospital stay, thus closing that chapter in my life.

The Puzzle

Every Sunday, John and I followed our usual routine. After a morning at church and a simple lunch at home, we settled on the couch to rest. While David and Rachel played, John watched football or graded his students' work, and I read the newspaper. Browsing through the *Quincy Herald Whig* one Sunday, I noticed a large advertisement for our local grocery store. The store was in a remodeling process that was due for completion in June 2004. As part of the festivities associated with the yearlong project, there would be a prize drawing in June.

To enter the contest, you had to faithfully check the paper every Sunday from September through May for puzzle pieces. With all the pieces collected and the puzzle taped together, the remodeled exterior of the building would be unveiled. By turning in the completed puzzle, you entered the drawing. The reward, a large sum of money, caught my attention. Gazing at the amount, I thought of all the ways that money could be used. Our 114-year-old house always needed repairs—a new roof, a new heating system, tuck-pointing the bricks, and the list went on. The decision was made; I was going to do this.

Each week, month after month, I grabbed the paper, looked for the advertisement, cut out my puzzle piece, and added it to the others. John was amused by my new routine.

With a smile on his face, he inquired, "Why are you doing this? You know the odds are against you. You're like a kid collecting Box Tops."

"You'll see," I said. "I'm going to win this money. Besides, it doesn't cost anything to enter but my time."

Once the year passed, I taped the puzzle pieces together, wrote my contact information on the back, and headed to the store.

Before dropping off the envelope, I prayed, "Lord, this money would be helpful to us. If it be Your will, may I please win?"

Several weeks later, I received a phone call. The store manager informed me that I was one of twenty-seven semi-finalists eligible for the grand prize. We were to meet at the store on Friday, June 11, for the final drawing.

I asked John, my in-laws, and my parents to join me in prayer that I might win. Later that week, I told the leaders from Wednesday morning Bible study that I was a finalist. Having served with these women for several years, they knew it wasn't typical for me to ask God for money. As we prayed together, these women fervently asked that I be awarded the money, and I made God a promise.

"Jesus," I prayed, "If you allow me to win this money, I

promise that I'll give You all the credit and glory."

Before long, my friends' prayers turned to praise and thanksgiving for our God who provides. I left that morning with hugs and congratulations and the belief that I was going to win.

Arriving Friday with John, David, and Rachel, we were ushered into a room with the other finalists and told the rules. Each of us would receive a raffle ticket with a number. The store manager would draw five tickets to determine who would make it to the final round.

As we waited to draw numbers, John stepped out of the room with our children for a trip to the bakery. He reentered as the last ticket was drawn and sadly shook his head, as if to say, "I'm sorry your ticket wasn't called." A large grin on my face, I held up my ticket to the finals.

At the front of the room were five large envelopes. The numbers on our ticket stubs determined the order we'd select our envelopes. Four people would win gift cards for the grocery store, leaving the grand prize for only one. When it was my turn, I saw two envelopes—number one and number four.

"Okay, God," I quickly prayed, "I'm choosing number one because You come first in my life."

As I picked it up, the elderly woman next to me reached for the other one. On the signal, all five of us tore into our packages. Struggling to get my envelope open, I saw that the other four people had gift cards in their hands. That meant that I was holding the grand prize—$10,000!

The look of disbelief on John's face was priceless. While people congratulated me, Lynn, the store manager, wrote my name on the oversized check. When the newspaper photographer walked over, I told him there was something I wanted printed in the paper. To their credit, the *Quincy Herald Whig* published exactly what I said.

"This is answered prayer," Coats said after winning the prize, adding that she planned to give some of the money to her church, pay off some bills and put the rest in a savings account. "I give all glory to Jesus Christ because He answered my prayers," she said.

You might say this is not a gift, but a prize. Or you might wonder what this had to do with my story of personal suffering. There was nothing I'd done to deserve that check. Nor was it something I'd named and claimed as my own. I believe God gave that to me as a gift. In His providence, He knew of an urgent need in the future—a need that I didn't even know about yet.

Remember the thousands of dollars we accumulated in bills from three emergency room visits, four hospital stays, doctor visits, surgery, procedures, tests, medications, and an ambulance ride? After a year of sitting in our savings account, that gift paid off all of those bills.

God's provision for us is marvelous.

As wonderful as that financial gift was, God blessed us even further. John and I developed a special relationship with Lynn, the store manager, and his sweet wife, Holly. We had many opportunities to spend time together—serving on Cursillo and Walk to Emmaus teams, studying Scripture on Tuesday evenings in our home, and fellowshipping when we got the chance.

The Second Gift
After my fourth hospital stay, I was finally on the road to recovery. A week after being released from the hospital, I received a phone call from my best friend. She told me that I needed to come to her house, that a gift had been delivered there for me. The gift was from Mary.

It had been eight months since Mary died; how could this

be? It turned out that Mary's son, while sorting through her things, came across a gift she'd purchased. The box, already wrapped, had a card attached to it with my name. Remembering where my friend lived, Mary's son delivered the gift to her house.

A beautiful silver cross hanging from three black leather strands lay in the little box. As I read the card, tears welled up in my eyes.

"Leigh Ann," it read, "the light of God's love shines through you and your every kindness. I shall never forget nor fail to appreciate that you walked beside me during the darkest part of my journey. Love, Mary."

Her words brought back my prayer about suffering from a year and a half earlier. God helped me stand with Mary in her grief. Even though I didn't know how to do it, He taught and guided me. I wear this special necklace often. It's a tangible symbol of my lessons in suffering, of the special woman sent to usher in these lessons, and of the great God we serve who works all things for good according to His purpose.

It all started with Mary. Unexpectedly, God brought her into my life and showed me the pathway into her pain. Walking beside her prepared me for my own physical suffering and gave the experience I needed in bearing one another's burdens and ministering to those who hurt.

Mary went to be with Jesus in July 2004. Every year after that, someone died in the small group I led at Wednesday Bible study. In 2005, it was a woman who lost her battle with cancer; many of her friends also attended the study. In 2006, a young woman whose mother and aunt were also in my group died unexpectedly one morning.

The many hours spent with Mary, learning about her grief and suffering, paved the way for me to care for others and share in their burdens. When my physical pain was removed, a surprise gift from Mary was a fitting closure to that season in my life.

Simple Gifts

Mary's gift was a simple expression of love, but it meant so much to me. As you have probably experienced, a gift doesn't need to be expensive to be a blessing. A handwritten letter, a flower, or a meal can lift your spirit in a wonderful way. And gifts don't have to be material. A kind or encouraging word or your time can be an invaluable gift to a person in need. Don't underestimate what God can do with your simple offering, no matter how small it may seem.

I often turn my love for cooking and baking into an opportunity to give. Many times, I'll make a double batch of whatever I'm cooking. A bread recipe might make three loaves, or a cake recipe might have three layers.

When there's extra, I ask God if someone needs the additional serving of food. Often a name comes quickly to mind. Repeatedly, God astonishes me at the greater purpose that He has behind a simple gift.

Having made an extra chicken pie years ago, I carefully fashioned a heart into the crust. God gave me Mary's name (yes, the same Mary you've been reading about). On Christmas Eve, my family surprised her with this gift. She later told me that it was just what she needed to nourish her body and her soul.

One Saturday evening, I had three freshly baked loaves of homemade bread when our pastor came to mind. That next morning, I laid one loaf on his desk with a note that read, "Dale, you're supposed to have this today. God bless." As the sermon was to begin, Dale laid the loaf on the pulpit.

"Our God is amazing!" he announced.

Dale's sermon that day was on Jesus, the Bread of Life. When leaving his home for church, Dale had grabbed a tiny piece of bread off the table for his sermon example, only to arrive and see a giant loaf sitting on his desk!

My family's favorite dessert is a homemade three-layer chocolate cake with icing that's so rich, it's almost like eating fudge. Because it is fully loaded with calories, I usually make one layer for us, and then share the others. On this particular day, August 27, God gave me two names: Damian and Lisa. When I appeared on their doorstep, we were all surprised. I didn't know that it was their twentieth wedding anniversary. They decided to have a quiet celebration with one another. In the midst of their work schedules, they didn't have a dessert—until then.

These were special examples when God gave me a name and allowed me to see how that gift was used. Whether we get to see the inner workings of God's plan or not, He can take our simple gifts and use them in far greater ways than we could imagine.

St. Augustine once said, "Find out how much God has given you and from it take what you need; the remainder is needed by others."[32] So, the next time you find yourself having more than you need, consider sharing the remainder with someone else. When giving a gift, ask God what He thinks about it. Maybe He has something in mind you hadn't considered.

Gifts are a channel of God's blessing.

Something to Consider
1. Who can you bless with an unexpected gift? Ask God to direct your gift giving.
2. What gift have you received that blessed you in abundance?

Why did it have that impact?

3. How has God taken what you thought was a simple gift to someone and turned it into something much greater?

Further Reflection
- Deuteronomy 16:17
- Acts 20:35
- 1 Timothy 6:18–19
- James 1:17

CHAPTER 14

KINDRED SPIRITS

Sitting in my closet is an English boarding trunk given to me by a Franciscan priest, a dear friend, who used the trunk during his travels abroad.

The box is special, but its contents make it valuable. It is filled with hundreds of cards and letters from people who have influenced my life and written words of encouragement and blessing to me. The letters come from family members and friends of all ages. They also come from various locations, often traveling from where I have lived or visited.

There are schoolteachers, professors, doctors, nurses, homebuilders, real-estate agents, stay-at-home mothers, administrators, pastors, priests, missionaries, store managers, engineers, social workers, musicians, attorneys, and students represented. They are Presbyterian, Catholic, Baptist, Church of God, Lutheran, Anglican, Non-Denominational, Mennonite, Congregational, Apostolic, Assembly of God, Methodist, and Pentecostal. Family members who shaped who I am today and friends who've endured divorce, miscarriage, cancer, wayward children, loneliness, and grief from losing loved ones. In this trunk are cards of encouragement from friends with whom

I've studied Scripture, prayed, laughed, shared meals with, and been accountable to. What is at the heart of this group? They all follow the same person, Jesus Christ.

Our relationships with those in this community of faith are the source of some of the greatest blessings we receive.

The Body of Christ ... the Church
It doesn't matter who we are, what our jobs are, or where we live. Members of the church come together with a shared calling—to belong to Jesus Christ. The church is not a physical building where people gather for worship, but is people who act as the hands, feet, and tongue of Christ. We are to live, work, travel, and speak as Christ would if He were in our shoes.

Romans 12:4–5 says, "For just as we have many members in one body and all the members do not have the same function, so we, who are many, are one body in Christ, and individually members one of another." Jesus is the head of the body, and each of us makes up a part of His spiritual body on earth. We have different functions, unique abilities, separate callings, and diverse locations.

In July 2002, while participating in a spiritual retreat, I sat in a chapel silently asking God to open my eyes and reveal what He wanted me to learn from the weekend. The Holy Spirit's answer was unexpected.

You've kept me in a "box" for too long, He said. *I'm going to show you the church like you have never seen it before. Let me introduce you to My body, the body of Christ.*

I didn't know what that meant or what to expect. I certainly didn't anticipate what happened later that evening during a candlelight worship service. Walking through crowds of people in the darkened chapel, I looked closely at each person's face. Seeing their smiles and hearing their voices united in song, I sensed God speaking to me.

Look at how beautiful and diverse My body is. It reaches

beyond age, denomination, race, culture, and socioeconomic status.

I wrote in my journal that evening,

> God has touched the depths of my soul tonight. I have always known in my mind that other believers were my brothers and sisters in Christ, but tonight, this has been etched in my heart and soul forever. This was my family standing there to welcome me, singing to our Jesus. I'm overwhelmed.

There are many ways that the church, the body of Christ, is beautifully diverse.

1. Generationally—Followers of Christ range from the little child to the elderly, and each one is important. Those who've walked with Jesus for a long time have much to pass on to younger believers—wisdom, life experience, and sound advice. Equally important are the small children who have such simple faith. They believe and accept Jesus for who He is and what He has done.

2. Spiritual Maturity—The church includes those who've known Jesus for a lifetime and those who've known Him just a few days. They walk with bold confidence, quiet doubts, uncontained zeal, or reserved wonder. Some know Scripture forward and backward while others are just learning. Regardless of where a believer is on the path to spiritual maturity, we all need each other.

3. Denominationally—God's church universal goes beyond the walls of denominations. When we humbly interact with people from other denominations, learn about different worship styles, examine our own personal beliefs, and compare those to what Scripture teaches, we grow as followers of Jesus.

4. Racially—The church is a kaleidoscope of races. God

does not distinguish who is His by skin color. Galatians 3:28 says, "There is neither Jew nor Greek, there is neither slave nor free man, there is neither male nor female; for you are all one in Christ Jesus." Skin color just shows the creativity of our God who made us in His image.

    5. Culturally—The body of Christ is made up of people from all over the world—different cultures, each with its own way of doing things. We may speak different languages, have unique accents, eat diverse foods, and live in different houses, but we all serve the same Lord and Savior. I have believing friends from Australia, Taiwan, England, China, Ecuador, and Chile. I also have missionary friends serving in China, Russia, and Vietnam. To hear how God is working in their lives and around the world enriches my faith.

    6. Socioeconomically—The church consists of people from various backgrounds and upbringings—rich, poor, blue collar, white collar, working/middle/upper class. We know from Scripture that God has a special place in His heart for the poor, widowed, orphaned, and needy. We also see those who've been gifted with wealth use their resources to help others.

    7. Politically—This is a sensitive point for many, but my brothers and sisters in Christ are members of the Republican, Democratic, and other political parties. Regardless of our different political views, we are still part of this spiritual family.

    8. Personalities—Peaceful, strong-willed, reserved, temperamental, laid-back, serious, high strung, joy-filled, melancholy, spirited, pessimistic, funny, doubtful, impulsive, and loving—these adjectives describe personalities in this community of faith. Look at some of the early followers of Jesus. Peter was impulsive, Thomas was skeptical, Paul was passionate, Philip was obedient, Barnabas was an encourager, and Luke was meticulous. God can take our strengths and weaknesses, our pasts and presents, so we can serve Him more fully with our futures.

9. Uniquely Gifted—Each member of the body of Christ has been given special gifts by the Holy Spirit for the purpose of building up the church. These gifts of grace include wisdom, knowledge, faith, healing, miracles, prophecy, discerning spirits, speaking in tongues, interpretation of tongues, serving, teaching, encouraging, giving, leading, and showing mercy.[33] Not everyone will have the same gift, and some may have more than others. Nonetheless, they are all important.

10. Not Bound by Time—The church refers to all who follow Christ, without respect to time. That means that believers—since creation—make up the body of Christ. There will come a day when all of Jesus's followers will finally be gathered together in one place—the new heaven, new earth, and the new Jerusalem (Revelation 21–22).

God broadened my perspective about His church the night of the retreat and that following year. John and I taught and attended several Bible studies from different denominational perspectives. However, God exploded our ministry opportunities, all of which crossed denominational lines. Interacting with so many church backgrounds challenged us to know what we did and did not believe and sharpened our ability to discuss our faith in Jesus Christ. It was a time of rich spiritual growth. Looking back, I recognize this as part of God's plan for us.

The Church, Alive and Active

Hopefully by now you have a good picture of who makes up the church. Having answered who makes up the church, we turn to answer the why and the what questions.

Why is the church important in our lives? What does the church actually do?

The purpose of the church is to glorify, enjoy, and worship God. These actions are incorporated in all the church does, every day of the week in everything we do, both individually and corporately.

To glorify God means to magnify Him through praising and honoring Him. It's being mindful of and knowing all He has accomplished in our lives. It's believing that Jesus died for us and therefore, we belong to Him. Because of our love and devotion for Him and His Son, we, in turn, endeavor to enjoy and worship Him in all we say and do.

Let us look at the role of the church in the believer's life.

1. To tell others the good news of Jesus. Oftentimes, we leave this to pastors, evangelists, and missionaries, when we're all commanded to share the good news with others. Don't know what to say? Tell people what God has done in your life personally through His Son, Jesus Christ, a story that begins 2,000 years ago. Through the sharing of your story, point them to the gospel message of Jesus.

2. To build one another up with our gifts and talents. As noted earlier, every follower of Christ has unique spiritual gifts and talents for the purpose of encouraging others and building up the body of Christ. Each member has some special way to contribute. Some will have the jobs of teaching, preaching, or counseling. Others will lead, plan, or perform administrative tasks. Many will serve quietly behind the scenes, taking care of children, sweeping floors, or changing light bulbs. Each role is significant; they all work together to accomplish "kingdom business."

3. To comfort and help one another. We can minister by extending comfort to others in time of need or distress. This may come in the form of a listening ear and quiet presence, or it may be a letter, phone call, or hug. Sometimes, talking about difficulties with which we struggle may reassure those with the same struggles. It is encouraging to know we are not alone; someone else knows how we feel (2 Corinthians 1:3–5).

4. To hold one another accountable. It's good to have a trustworthy believer hold you accountable and speak truth to you in love. Many miss the benefits of accountability. Accountability can help you fight temptation, remind or encourage you to accomplish a certain task, and call you to a higher standard. Regardless, when we speak truth into one another's lives (as seen in Ephesians 4:15), it facilitates spiritual growth.

5. To share with one another. Part of the job of the church is to fellowship, worship, sing, eat, study, and pray together, and there's nothing like companionship with fellow believers. It nourishes and enriches the soul. God knows that we need each other and told us in Hebrews 10:25 to not give up meeting together, but encourage one another. Spending time with others reminds us that we're not alone, nor should we go it alone.

6. To study Scripture together. It is life enriching to sit among the church and dig into God's Word together. Learn from the insights that others have. A different perspective challenges us to look more closely at Scripture. When questions arise, another may have an answer or explanation; if not, search God's Word together.

7. To pray for one another. Interceding for one another in prayer is imperative. It's a rich blessing to pray for others and see how God answers. Sometimes answers come quickly. Other times it takes years. And sometimes we won't see God's answer in our lifetime. Regardless of how that works out, it's a privilege to take requests to God on behalf of another—asking, expecting, and looking for the answer. This is a vital ministry of the church.

8. To promote unity. As a body of believers, we're to work together, regardless of our different personalities, likes, and dislikes. Extending love to each other promotes unity. Love, according to Colossians 3:14, is the perfect bond of unity. Jesus desired this unity among believers. In His high priestly prayer in John 17:20–21, Jesus prayed that those who believed in Him would be one, unified together, just as Jesus is One with the Father and the Spirit.

The Treasure of a Friend
In the midst of this faith community, God gifts us with close, intimate friends. These relationships are extra special because of the level of trust, sharing, and commitment involved. Jesus was surrounded by people much of the time. Among these crowds, He had a unique relationship with His twelve disciples who were His friends. Even then, Peter and the two brothers James and John were His very closest companions. These three disciples were with Jesus in some of His most intimate moments, being at the transfiguration of Jesus when Moses and Elijah appeared and God spoke aloud, and in the garden of Gethsemane where Jesus prayed the night before His crucifixion.

Time spent with close Christian friends makes you a better person. Author and counselor H. Norman Wright best describes the experience had with these types of friends.

> In a friendship relationship you will come to a greater understanding of who you are in Christ and as a person. When you engage in intimate sharing and experience transparency, your facades drop away, and you learn to confront who you really are in a new way. One of the blessings of friendship is personal growth and growth as a follower of Christ.[34]

Unity, oneness with Christ, a bond of love—those are words for kindred spirits. We experience this kinship with Jesus and other members of the church when we spend time together. That takes effort on our part and needs to be a priority if we are to experience the benefits and blessings of being part of the church.

Are you a believer in Christ trying to go it alone without your local church? You are missing out! It would be as if you took all those letters from my treasure chest and read them repeatedly, allowing that to be your only involvement with your brothers and sisters in Christ. You reread their words, replay memories, and remember times spent together, but never interact with them in person.

You can read your Bible and pray at home, and you should. However, being isolated from the church is unhealthy spiritually. We're strongest when we work together. There may be a person who is supposed to minister to you; better yet, maybe you're supposed to reach out to someone. Either way, you both miss out.

Are you not in a local church for other reasons? Did someone hurt you or neglect to pay attention to you? Forgive that person and move on. Find a different local church to attend if necessary. Just remember, the church is made up of sinners who have been redeemed, and you're one of them. None of us are perfect. There will be flaws, mistakes, and other unfortunate circumstances inside every congregation. The head of the church is Jesus, who can overcome all of that.

Don't choose to go it alone. Some of your richest experiences in life come through those who share faith in Jesus Christ.

**The community of believers, the church,
is a channel of God's blessing.**

Something to Consider
1. Are you experiencing and receiving God's blessing through the ministry of others in your community of faith? How?
2. How are you being a blessing to others in your church?
3. Who prays for and with you? Who encourages you? With whom do you share and discuss spiritual truths? If no one fulfills these roles, why not, and what can you do to find friends to help you in these ways?

Further Reflection
- Ecclesiastes 4:12
- Romans 12:4–5
- Colossians 3:14–15
- Hebrews 10:24–25

CHAPTER 15
"YOU WANT ME TO DO WHAT?"

Your comfort zone is a pleasant place to be. It offers security, familiarity, and confidence. When clothing fits, it puts you at ease. Laying your head on your own pillow is soothing; sinking into a soft chair is luxurious; sitting by a warm fire is calming.

We like to be comfortable. How nice if we could keep things that way. But when change comes, it often takes us out of that comfort zone and brings with it the unknown. We may feel weak or vulnerable, but these times are ripe for God's transforming work.

An Unexpected Command
During my last hospital stay in Quincy, it seemed I was in a recurring bad dream. Clothed in a hospital gown, an IV in my arm, lying in bed, I awaited yet another procedure. Apprehension clouded my face.

"Lord," I asked, "is there something I haven't learned yet that I'm here in the hospital a fourth time?"

In the quiet, I heard in my spirit, *Write it down.*

"What? Write what?"

Again, I heard those same three words. *Write it down.*

"Lord! You want me to do what? I know I heard you wrong. Are you saying You want me to write a book? Sorry, but this Gideon girl is going to need You to show me that I heard you correctly."

A week after being released from the hospital, I shared some of the ways God had been working in my life with numerous people, only to have them say, "Have you ever thought of writing that down?"

After hearing this question numerous times, my response was finally, "Yeah, actually I have."

You could hear my feet dragging by the tone of my voice. I turned to God in prayer and submitted in the best way I knew.

"Okay, Lord," I said. "I'll do it."

Slowly, my God stories found their way onto paper.

Several months later I heard my name called around three a.m., while lying in bed awake.

Leigh Ann.

I considered Samuel in the Old Testament and echoed his words when God called. "Yes Lord, here I am."

Write it down. Call it A Blessed Life. *Base it on John 1:16.*

I jumped out of bed, grabbed my Bible, and ran into the study where I wrote His words on a blue Post-it note. John 1:16 was unfamiliar, so I looked it up and sat in awe. "From the fullness of his grace we have all received one blessing after another" (NIV). God does the most incredible things!

While I was amazed at God's provision, writing a book wasn't on my to-do list. The task of putting thoughts into words for people to read was daunting and overwhelming. However, time and again, I was reminded that the Lord directs my steps (see Proverbs 16:9). God used this manuscript to change my life, changes I'll elaborate on in the next chapter.

Change on the Horizon

After hearing God's voice, a year went by with little writing. Having lived in Quincy for almost ten years, our lives were full of close friends, thriving ministries, a great church, steady employment, and fun activities for our children. My life was so active that I was increasingly busy, tired, and weighed down. I lacked intimacy and time with God. How was I to be obedient and write in addition to all my other responsibilities?

By 2006, my stress manifested physically. I lost my voice and couldn't sing or teach well, and what appeared to be a pinched nerve in my shoulder and neck disabled my left hand, making it difficult to play the piano. My friend, an ear, nose, and throat doctor, couldn't find a medical reason why I'd lost my voice.

At this point, God had my full attention. I told Him how I struggled.

"Lord," I prayed, "what I really want is intimacy with You, to sit at Your feet. It's also my desire to be obedient in writing, but I have no time. I'll give up whatever You want me to so that this can be accomplished."

A week after praying this, John came home from work for lunch. Following our meal, he slid a piece of paper across the table for me to see. On it was a job description for a history professor at Lee University in Cleveland, Tennessee. We weren't looking to move and were content to remain in Quincy, so it took me by surprise. Reading through the ad, it struck me how perfectly John fit the description. Teaching history at an intentionally Christian liberal arts university was his dream job.

Then I remembered what I'd told God: "I'll give up whatever You want me to give up."

His answer was to move us, to give up Quincy. I was strangely relieved that I didn't have to choose what activities to relinquish.

John expected me to balk at the idea of a move, but I didn't.

"John, I said, "I think we need to pray about this. It appears God is getting ready to move us to Tennessee."

As John prepared his application, I made a giant moving list—packing supplies, school and medical files, getting the house ready to sell, and transitioning out of our activities and passing the baton to others.

John reminded me frequently that he hadn't even applied for the job yet, to which I said, "Not yet, but you will."

Finally, the day to mail the application came. Sitting in the post office parking lot, I prayed over the envelope, asking God for clear direction. Were we to move from Quincy? This huge leap of faith would bring change in every way for our family.

We often miss when God is working in our lives. A major event occurs, time elapses, and several years later we reflect on the past, coming to the conclusion that God was behind the scenes, weaving together what originally appeared to be coincidence. However, this go around, John and I were aware of God directing what was happening. There was a heightened sensitivity to God's divine intervention. Steven Curtis Chapman's song "Dive" became our theme song over the next five months. The lyrics best described what we were encountering.

> I have been carried here to where the river flows
> My heart is racing and my knees are weak as I walk to the edge
> I know there is no turning back
> Once my feet have left the ledge
> And in the rush I hear a voice
> That's telling me it's time
> To take the leap of faith
> So here I go
> I'm diving in, I'm going deep, in over my head, I want to be
> Caught in the rush, lost in the flow, in over my head,
> I want to go.[35]

We were in the center of a supernatural current. From January to May 2006, we experienced God in many ways.

- After mailing the application, I stood in the kitchen eating carryout Chinese food. Eyeing the fortune cookie on the counter, I jokingly asked God if He placed an answer about the move in my cookie. Curiosity took over. When I snapped the cookie in half, this message dropped out: "Your life will soon take you down a new path. Enjoy the trip!" God can be playful.
- In February, our family traveled to Chattanooga, Tennessee, for an extended weekend and to scout the nearby campus of Lee University. The children, who were ages ten and six, enjoyed the Tennessee Aquarium, eating out, seeing the mountains, and hanging out at the hotel (it was still winter in Tennessee!).

Driving thirty miles east to Cleveland, we heard David from the back seat say, "This place is great! I could live here."

"Funny you should say that David," I replied, "as that may be exactly what happens." We explained to our children the possibility of a move. David's comment was yet another confirmation.

- John had a telephone interview at the end of February. My unwavering confidence that we were moving to Cleveland continued to alternately baffle and amuse my husband. I believe God enjoyed seeing this all played out and how we reacted to His unexpected surprises. After a quick dinner run to Taco Bell, I returned home and handed out the food. As the children laughed at the messages on their sauce packets, I noticed John staring at his and discovered that ours both said the same thing—"Willing to relocate." Over the years, we've checked all our Taco Bell packets, but have never seen this message again.
- God literally replaced John and me in our jobs and ministries. People stepped up or moved to town at just the right

time. It was fascinating to watch this take place. Every "coincidence" was evidence that God was providentially working in the details of our lives and preparing us for this move.

While the changes were intriguing, they were also unsettling. After Bible study one Wednesday, I shared these thoughts with my pastor. My friend gently spoke the truth in love to me.

"You know, Leigh Ann," he said. "You are not irreplaceable."

That was exactly what I needed to hear. God would continue working His purposes in those jobs and ministries in Quincy. We didn't need to be there for that to happen.

- John received an on-campus interview, and in April, he was offered the job at Lee. Trying to process how quickly this was all happening wasn't easy; knowing that our house was going on the market made my heart sad. Loaded down with boxes and packing tape, I struggled to open the back door, only to be stopped by an elderly couple who had questions about the Governor's mansion next to our house.

During the course of our conversation, it came up that we were moving. Because of their frequent moves, they imparted many encouraging words that lifted my spirit. After getting into their car to leave, the man got back out and walked over to me.

"You know," he said, pointing at me, "you have no idea what friends God has waiting for you in Cleveland, Tennessee."

As he and his wife drove off, I stood staring after them. I don't remember mentioning that we were moving to Cleveland. Had I just entertained angels unaware? What did God have for me in this new city?

- The day our Quincy house went on the market, we received two offers. During the previous months, John and I browsed the Cleveland real-estate websites. We found a house that we loved, but it was out of our price range. On a return trip to Cleveland, we searched for two days trying to find the right house. The last house the real-estate agent showed us was the house we'd fallen in love with. Walking into it, we knew it was perfect for our needs. Our offer was accepted that day at a price we could afford.

- By the end of May, reality set in that serious change was happening—the hardest of which was leaving our friends. They loved on us, prayed over us, fed us, and threw parties and dinners for us. The month-and-a-half long farewell was like attending our own wake. Our friends voiced their thoughts to us in person, before groups, through gifts, and in letters and cards. It is humbling to have such loving friends. That was a bittersweet time. Difficult in many ways, but some of the sweetest memories that I cherish.

The move to Cleveland went well. Our family enjoyed a delightful summer together exploring our new city and the nearby mountains. In August, John and the children started school. My world completely changed.

And Now for Something Completely Different
Before leaving Quincy, close friends gave us a lovely piece of artwork that hangs in our stairwell. It features a beautiful tree and the verse, "Be still before the Lord and wait patiently for him...."[36] No one knew how appropriate that verse would be for my life in Tennessee.

My new companions in Cleveland were Solitude, Silence, and Stillness. Solitude—it was just the Lord and me for the better part of the day. Silence—it was so quiet, I became familiar with the creaks of the house, the sounds of nature, and my own breathing. Stillness waited patiently, as I struggled to adjust. That first year, I begged God to let me join two different women's Bible study groups, one in the fall and the other that following spring. I sensed His blessing and went. However, God had a condition.

You can go, but keep your mouth shut. Do NOT speak.

That was difficult. After leading Bible study for so many years, He wanted me to be quiet and listen. Stillness—God erased my schedule. He gave me my heart's desire to sit still at His feet, but the change was so drastic that it was difficult to cease moving, both in body and mind.

By my third year in Tennessee, as I was settling in with my "S" companions, a new one came along and took me by surprise—Sorrow.

I cried often and felt an incredible sense of loss. After many weeks of confusion and frustration, I became concerned something was wrong with me. Being confident and at peace with where God had moved us, I asked God what was going on. When the Holy Spirit spoke, His words were a soothing balm to my soul.

You are grieving.

What a relief to have a name for my unsettling condition. I had lost the body of Christ in Quincy—worshiping, praying, ministering, studying Scripture, and fellowshipping together. Someone once told me that grief is a statement confirming that you loved someone. I left behind many friends in Quincy who were like family to me, people I love deeply.

Life would not be the same as it was, but God can work all things to the good of those who love him (Romans 8:28). The fact that it's going to be different is hard, but okay. It's in those situations that we create a new normal.

H. Norman Wright writes,

> Grief can awaken a strength, a dormant talent, a never used ability, a never before discovered perspective on life, a new sense of compassion for the struggles and hurts of others, or a new relationship with God. A time of good-bye forces us to make a change in our life and discover what is unfinished within us.[37]

As I began my sixth year in Cleveland, I continued to be amazed at how God worked in and through these huge changes. God knew the environment I needed to accomplish the task of writing a book.

Our house was on a quiet street where birds love to sing. My open schedule allowed me time to think and write. There were three houses in a row directly across the street from ours. One neighbor wrote and published a devotional book about how God worked in her life. Next door to her was a retired pastor who wrote and published a book on suffering and how God reveals Himself through our pain. Right next to his house was yet another neighbor who had her writings published in magazines and hoped to publish her novel. On numerous occasions, she encouraged me in my own writing, gave me helpful advice, and introduced me to new thoughts and ideas.

The presence of these three writers is not coincidental, but these providential incidents are further evidence that God cares enough about me to be deeply involved in the details of my life. I've only scratched the surface of the ways that God has worked through the changes brought on by our move.[38]

Change—a Necessary Part of Life
Change happens. No matter how hard we try to stop it, our bodies age. We can nip it, tuck it, dye it, and tone it, but we cannot prevent the inevitable. We shouldn't be discouraged by this fact. This body is temporary and isn't meant to last forever. Followers of Jesus Christ are reassured that we'll one day receive new eternal bodies. Talk about a real change!

I recognize that God doesn't always "dot every i and cross every t" as He did during our recent season of change. But God is with us in all the details. God showed Himself to us during our move as a confirmation that it was the right choice and what He desired for us. He knew the trials I'd face in our new hometown and how difficult change would be. Knowing without a shadow of a doubt that God wanted our family in Tennessee gave me great assurance and confidence. So when those challenging days came, I persevered, knowing that God had a plan.

What happens when change comes and we don't see God at all? A house doesn't sell, a spouse dies suddenly, unanswered questions trouble us, a job is lost, a diagnosis is made. Difficult circumstances cause us to come to grips with change, especially unwelcome change. That's where faith in an all-knowing God is essential. We grab onto Him, hold tight, and trust Him. We cling to His Word and the encouragement it gives us, such as that found in Romans 5:3–5, which says, "we also exult in our tribulations, knowing that tribulation brings about perseverance; and perseverance, proven character; and proven character, hope; and hope does not disappoint, because the love of God has been poured out within our hearts through the Holy Spirit who was given to us."

Change can be synonymous with tribulation. Read those same verses above, replacing the word *tribulation* with *change*. God does not change, nor do His promises in the Bible. Because of this, we can face change and not be fearful. Through our endurance and perseverance, we learn, grow, and allow the Holy Spirit to transform us.

Are you in a season of change? Rest in the knowledge that God is sovereign. He's in control and cares about what you're going through!

Change is a channel of God's blessing.

Something to Consider
1. Why is change so scary? Why do we fight it rather than face it head on?
2. Share a time when you experienced a significant change. What lessons did you learn?
3. When have you needed to persevere during a season of change? How has that built your character? How did God reveal Himself to you during that time?

Further Reflection
- Joshua 1:9
- John 1:16
- Romans 5:3–5
- Hebrews 13:8

CHAPTER 16

"HELP ME, LORD, I AM SICK OF MYSELF!"

There's an old saying that goes something like this—"Be careful what you ask for; you just might get it!" By praying boldly, I've grown into the belief that when you genuinely ask God for big things and have great expectations of Him, He answers in big ways.

I see my prayers as telling God what is in my heart and on my mind. They're sincere words spoken to God, without always realizing exactly what I am saying.

- Meet me in my dreams.
- Allow me to take someone else's burden.
- God, please reign on Halloween.
- Slow me down that I may see You this Easter weekend.
- Teach me about suffering.
- Lord, who needs a gift today?
- I want to spend time with You, but I'm so busy.
- I'll give up whatever You want me to give up.

You'll recall how God responded to these innocent questions and comments with extraordinary and sometimes supernatural answers. God in His wisdom does things in a different way than I envision, yet I trust Him because He is trustworthy.

So often, we ask God for something and discount His ability to look ahead in our lives and know exactly what we need. We ask at surface level, and God's answers go far deeper. I pray, telling God I'll do whatever He wants me to do, and unexpectedly find myself holding a friend whose daughter has just died. I pray, asking God for more time to sit at His feet, only to encounter an empty schedule brought about by a new job in a new location. After enough of these lessons, I've learned that it's okay to anticipate God accomplishing great things in my life, even if it's not through the means I'd expect or choose.

Praying this way carries a sense of adventure and suspense. It also bears the distinct possibility that God may have something else in mind that I hadn't considered.

Author Eugene Peterson says,

> Praying puts us at risk of getting involved with God's conditions. . . . Praying most often doesn't get us what we want but what God wants, something quite at variance with what we conceive to be in our best interests. And when we realize what is going on, it is often too late to go back.[39]

The word *risk* can have negative connotations, but that's not the case here. Any danger or threat perceived is from our perspective, especially if there's the possibility that we might have to give up control. When praying, it's as if God responds by altering the terms of our prayer to give us something far better than we asked for.

Seeing Yourself for Whom You Really Are

In August 2006, having been in Cleveland for just a few months, I settled down on my screened-in porch and began this book-writing adventure. Much thought was given on how to wisely approach this new task. Having an attitude of prayer seemed an excellent way to start, so I asked a group of family and friends to pray for me on a regular basis while I wrote. They would hold me accountable during the writing process. I decided to use the month of August as a time of preparation between God and me. The majority of my morning and afternoon hours were spent in prayer and Bible study.

During this time, I asked God to remove anything that hindered our relationship. Intimacy with the Lord is my heart's desire and has been my prayer for years. Like David in Psalm 19:12, I pleaded for God to reveal to me any hidden sin or fault of which I was unaware, so I could confess my sin.

"Show me my sin" is a bold prayer. I'm rarely disappointed with God's answers—sometimes taken aback, often surprised, but not disappointed. So it didn't strike me that I'd invited God to do some serious work in my life spiritually. I'm a pretty good person, right? Surely He didn't have too many things to point out. How mistaken I was!

Leaving that request at God's feet, I put pen to paper. I enjoyed two years of successful writing, turning out twelve chapters. The topic of each chapter lead me toward happy words and thoughts that made me feel good. But in November 2008, things began to change. God introduced the idea of writing about surrender, and I didn't like that. Then new chapter suggestions were put forward: humility, gratitude, and forgiveness. Writing about what I wanted to write versus what God wanted me to write became a spiritual battle.

After much resistance, I shelved the manuscript, along with my time with God. In spite of my childish disobedience and lack of submission, God continued to persist and pursue. He reminded me through Scripture that He loved me and that I was His. After several months of struggling, I surrendered and wrote the chapter entitled "I Am Not My Own."

I think a lot about God's refining fire in Zechariah 13:9. God allowed the heat to be turned up in my life, thus exposing the sins that hinder intimacy between us. He started with a big one—pride. I struggle with pride, doing things my way and thinking my time is mine to do with as I please.

We moved from there to pride partnered with selfishness. My desires, my feelings, my time, my stuff . . . me, me, me. Through prayer and Scripture, God showed me things about my actions, attitudes, thoughts, and time that didn't honor Him.

And He brought to light another situation that grieved my heart. More than twenty years earlier, a relationship with a close friend went awry. For years I had recurrent dreams about this particular individual, dreams that left me perplexed. When I'd wake up, I'd pray for him. One day, I sat at my desk with my head in my hands, trying to figure out what went wrong.

In my frustration, I told God, "I just don't get it. Why did our friendship end? What was his problem?"

The familiar voice of the Holy Spirit whispered two heartbreaking words to my soul: *You were.*

It was if a video camera played in my head, showing thoughtless and insensitive words said many years ago. I could blame it on immaturity, which I'm sure played a part. However, even then, I knew better than to speak with little consideration. I didn't heed the advice given to me as a child, "Think before you speak." Oh, to have the opportunity to go back and make a wrong right!

Convicted, I apologized to this person, decades after the offense. It was difficult, but necessary. Because he has forgiven me, our relationship is reconciled. His forgiveness is a gift, as is his friendship.

It's unsettling to catch sight of your true sinful self—who you really are. Walls collapse, the facade drops, and what you see is what you get. It's transparency and vulnerability at its best. Philip Yancey points out that

God already knows who we are; we are the ones who must find a way to come to terms with our true selves. Psalm 139 cried out, "Search me, O God. . . . See if there is any offensive way in me." In order to overcome self-deception, I need God's all-knowing help in rooting out hidden offenses like selfishness, pride, deceit, and lack of compassion.[40]

Likewise, Ruth Haley Barton beautifully describes this process of self-knowledge.

This willingness to see ourselves as we are and to name it in God's presence is at the very heart of the spiritual journey. But it takes time, time to feel safe enough with ourselves and with God to risk exposing the tender, unfinished places of the soul. We are so accustomed to being shamed or condemned in the unfinished parts of ourselves that it is hard to believe there is a place where all of who we are—the good, the bad, and the ugly—will be handled with love and gentleness.[41]

God is the ultimate gentleman. Reflecting back on my own experience, God was loving when He answered my prayer. He didn't call attention to my sins right away, but disclosed them to me slowly over time. He knew when those sins were brought to light, I'd face a gamut of emotions, for I felt raw and naked.

I trust God with all my insecurities, for He is loving, gentle, compassionate, and forgiving. Besides, He already knows me better than I know myself.

The Path of Humility
Being brought low has given me cause to consider the Biblical concept of humility. While contemplating this topic, I found that humility is:

- Surrendering everything to Jesus and giving permission for Him to be our all (Titus 2:11–14, Acts 17:25–28, 1 Corinthians 15:28).
- Recognizing our wretched state before our holy God. Seeing ourselves as we really are and understanding that self has not one good thing in it, except serving as an empty vessel for God to fill (Isaiah 64:6, Romans 3:23 and 7:18, 2 Timothy 2:21).
- Knowing that we can do nothing apart from Jesus Christ; only God can meet our desperate need (John 15:5).
- Admitting that nothing we've done merits our salvation in Jesus Christ—it is a gift of God (Romans 6:23, Titus 3:4–7).
- Seeing ourselves decrease that He may increase—less of me, more of Christ (John 3:30).
- Having a servant's attitude that focuses on others rather than on ourselves (Philippians 2:3).
- Being content with weakness so that God can be our strength (2 Corinthians 12:9–10).
- Comprehending that we really have no control over our future; only our Sovereign God does (James 4:14–15).
- Being willing to examine ourselves regularly with God's help to determine where we fall short, then confessing to God and turning away from those very sins (2 Corinthians 13:5, Jeremiah 12:3, 1 John 1:9).

To see perfect humility we need not look further than Jesus Christ, who encourages us to follow His example. "Learn from Me," He says, "for I am gentle and humble in heart..." (Matthew 11:29). He demonstrates what humility looks like when He repeatedly says that He can do nothing apart from His Father. His ultimate act of humility was seen on the cross, when "He humbled Himself by becoming obedient to the point of death, even death on a cross" (Philippians 2:8).

Humility teaches the importance of becoming nothing, so

that He might become everything. Jesus taught through His sermons to deny ourselves, take up our cross daily, and follow Him. He goes on to say whoever loses his life for His sake will save it (Luke 9:23–24). The Apostle Paul preaches, "I have been crucified with Christ; and it is no longer I who live, but Christ lives in me; and the life which I now live in the flesh I live by faith in the Son of God, who loved me and gave Himself up for me" (Galatians 2:20).

Dying to self is a daily, life-long process, in which God works in me through His Son, Jesus, and His Spirit that dwells in me.

Seeing Yourself as God Says You Are
As God brought my sins out in the open, I felt immense sorrow and disgust. Just looking in the mirror caused me to be irritable, grouchy, and downright belligerent.

There's a warning here! You must be careful not to wallow in self-despair when seeing how wretched you are apart from God. The devil would love for you to remain in an ongoing pity party.

"Woe is me. I'm pathetic. I'm unworthy. I'm just a worm. There's no good in me. How can anybody put up with me? I sure can't!"

God doesn't want you to live in this miserable state. Being aware of your transgressions is not the end of the process; it's a step on the way. It's humbling to have God expose your ugly, sinful nature, but He does that for His children—especially when they ask Him to do so.

He remained by my side as I worked through this wearisome time, sending me reminders of His love, extending His grace, and granting forgiveness. Andrew Murray's words resonated with my own experience.

> The more abundant the experience of grace the more in-

tense the consciousness of being a sinner. It is not sin, but God's grace showing a man and ever reminding him what a sinner he was that will keep him truly humble. It is not sin but grace that will make me know myself as a sinner.[42]

God reminds us of our sin for our good and for making us holy. Holiness is God's work, remaking us in character and attitude, so that we reflect the image of our Savior, Jesus Christ.

J.I. Packer describes it as God shaking us free of "all that displeases the Father, dishonors the Son, and grieves the Holy Spirit, so as to honor God more."[43]

He knows this refining process hurts, but He also knows it's essential. If we fail to recognize our sinfulness, then we fall short in appreciating the enormous sacrifice of Jesus on the cross.

In His ultimate act of humility, Jesus opened the door for us to become His brothers and sisters, adopted into the family of God. As believers in Christ, we belong to God. He gives us a new identity. Yes, He knows that we are sinners, but our old nature that relishes sin is no more—it has passed away. We've become new people (2 Corinthians 5:17).

Scripture uses a variety of expressions to describe our new identity: friend, saint, child, son/daughter, citizen of heaven, witness, elect, royalty, bride of the Lamb, minister, God's temple, ambassador, heir, co-worker with Christ, God's workmanship, His possession. And the Bible also lists adjective after adjective to describe this new nature in Christ. We are new, alive, adopted, forgiven, redeemed, holy, complete, free, anointed, assured, sealed, loved, justified, established, godly, righteous, salt, light, chosen, and treasured.

When God looks at this new you, this is what He sees! And then, He uses my favorite expression, "You are Mine!"[44] Knowledge of this should stir your soul; it does mine.

There's a relentless battle between viewing ourselves as God sees us and viewing ourselves as the world sees us. While living in Quincy, others saw me as David and Rachel's mom, Dr. Coats's wife (at least the college students called me that), parent volunteer, friend, hostess, church member, preschool music teacher, voice instructor, Bible teacher (one group called me the Bible Lady), prayer partner, and the herb/flower lady. These labels, which are accurate and good things in and of themselves, became my identity.

When I moved to Tennessee, I had an identity crisis. As John and I met people, I was impatient to tell them who I was and what I was capable of doing.

God quickly brought that to an end with a clear command: *Stop that!* After years of talking, going, and doing, God wanted me to be quiet, still, and ready to listen.

During a conversation with a friend, she and I talked about the identities given to us.

"So, how do you see yourself?" she asked

"Well, that's easy," I replied quickly, "I'm His."

"Do you really see it that way?" she asked.

I did, and then my eyes opened. It was as if the Holy Spirit said, *Yes! That is what I've been telling you all these years. You finally got it. You are Mine!*

This was a direct answer to a prayer I wrote in my journal on January 12, 2009. "God, when will I fully learn that I am not my own?"

Over the course of four years, unbeknownst to me, God reshaped my identity. I had read those verses in Scripture so many times about my new nature in Christ that they slowly changed how I viewed myself.

Working on this book and being taught humility were the very avenues that God used to change my life for the better.

I've no doubt that in the next season of my life, God will have lessons awaiting me to further this spiritual transformation.

As long as you're on this earth, you're a work in progress. Don't let those other identities, including your old sinful nature, crowd out the one that matters most. If you are in Christ, you are His—a treasured possession of the One True God!

So if you're distressed by sin in your life and catch yourself crying out, "Help me, Lord, I am sick of myself!", know that you are in a position that is ripe for God's handiwork.

Allow Him to give you a picture of yourself—the good, the bad, and the ugly. Then prepare to walk the path of humility.

If you're upset and disgruntled by the thorns and the rocks that trip you, and if you grumble and say, "I can't do this," you're right. But hang in there! Take comfort in the knowledge that while you can't, God can. Give things over to Him, and He will enable you to do things you never dreamed of doing. He's ready to lavish His grace upon you and show you your true identity. When you are in Christ, you are a child of the King!

Humility is a channel of God's blessing.

Something to Consider
1. Why is it so difficult for us to be transparent with others? Do you find it easier to be real before God or people? Why?
2. If you were to paint a picture with your words, what would a person of humility look like?
3. What identities do people give you? Which do you tend to gravitate toward—your old sinful nature or your new identity in Christ? How can knowing who you are in Jesus Christ bring freedom?

Further Reflection
- Psalm 139:1–24
- Zechariah 13:9
- Matthew 6:5–8
- John 15:5

CHAPTER 17

WHICH ONE WILL IT BE?

When we witness or hear about extraordinary incidents, we have to ask, "Providence or coincidence, which one will it be?"

The kitchen door closed a little harder than normal. John, standing on the doormat with his shoulders slumped, let out a long sigh. Something was amiss. I wracked my brain to figure out what went wrong so quickly. Dinner was finished, the children were playing, and John had taken the trash out. Everything was in order, except for the expression on my husband's face.

"My ring is missing."

His comment was followed by another sigh, this time from me.

This wouldn't be the first time John lost his wedding ring; actually, this was the latest in a long string of incidents. He'd lost his wedding ring in the inner recesses of a chair, found it in the bottom of his dress shoe, and discovered it hanging on his belt rack.

"Keep your cool," I told myself. "He looks genuinely upset

about this. Watch your tone of voice, girl."

To John's credit, the loss was truly accidental. It was a winter evening in Illinois, and the sun had just gone down. It was extremely cold, the sort of cold that comes with wind chill advisories and causes ring fingers to shrink. His ring slipped off his finger and landed somewhere in the grass of our big yard.

Keeping my voice in check, I said, "You know we have to find it. Tonight."

In other words, "Everything is going to come to a complete halt, mister, until you get out there and find that missing ring!"

When an item is lost in our household, something happens. I become a woman single-minded on finding that one thing. John calls it "obsessed." I like to call it "determined."

Either way, the hunt was on.

Wearing his heavy coat and thick gloves and toting a flashlight, John headed into the cold night. An hour later, he returned to the kitchen aggravated, without the ring.

Thus began a torrent of thoughts running through my mind. "Oh, this will not do! That is unacceptable. Let me have the flashlight; I'll find it myself!"

Pulling on my coat and gloves and grabbing the car keys, I took over the search-and-rescue mission. I turned on both of our vehicles, so the lights would shine on our yard. The flashlight would take care of the rest. After an hour of traipsing through the grass and patches of snow (yes, I forgot to mention the snow), I hadn't made any more progress than John.

Refusing to go back into the house and admit defeat, I stood in the yard and weighed my options. First, get angry. I'd already accomplished that one. Second, cry, but that would make my nose run. Third, try again tomorrow when it was light. However, that wasn't an option. The ring had to be found tonight. Fourth, pray, as talking to God is always good.

The gold band had great value to me. It signified the covenant John and I made before God and man. We promised to be faithful to one another and recognize Christ as the head of our home. Turning off the car lights and the flashlight, I picked the last option. I prayed.

As I stood in the middle of the backyard, the cold night grew dark, matching my mood. My conversation with God took an introspective turn as I walked through the yard again.

"God, it's so dark out here," I prayed. "There are so many people in this world who live in darkness, never hearing about Jesus Christ. You are the Light. Lord, thank You for Your light. Please shine Your radiance on this ring. I'm tired and looking to You for help. I'm encouraged when You say, 'Nothing is impossible with God.' You know where John's ring is."

I took a step and glanced down. The lamp from the kitchen window shone down to illuminate John's wedding ring directly in front of my right foot. I stood for a moment, processing. Then I dropped to my knees, thanking God for finding something lost, but mostly for the gift of His presence. Humbled, I entered the house, eager to share what God had done.

A week later, I was in the middle of another search. Earlier that morning, David's first grade teacher called from school with the news that David lost his brand new glasses while at recess (he has inherited some of his father's genes). After settling two-year-old Rachel at a friend's house, I headed to the elementary school to commence the search.

My remorseful son met me at his classroom door and put it in plain words. "The glasses are somewhere in the grass field where we play baseball," he said.

Sending David back to his desk, I trudged down the hallway. "Did he say the grass field? Are you kidding me?" I muttered under my breath. "Does he realize how big that baseball field is and how small his glasses are? Didn't I just do this one week ago with a ring?"

Outside in the cold, brisk air, I faced the expanse of what

was supposed to be the baseball field but was actually a pasture that hadn't been mowed in weeks. How was I supposed to find his glasses in that? Well, if this was going to be an impossible task, there was only one place to start.

"Lord, here I am again, looking for something that has been lost." I sighed. "You know where the glasses are. I have faith in You, God. You illuminated John's ring in the dark, so there's no doubt that you can reveal David's hidden glasses. Will You please show me where they are?"

I finished the prayer, took a few steps, and looked down. Right in front of my feet, lying in the weeds were David's little glasses. As I processed yet another immediate answer to prayer, I marveled at God's amazing kindness and generosity.

Waiting Expectantly

Would you say that finding my husband's ring and my son's glasses was providence or coincidence? When we experience these remarkable situations, words like *fate*, *chance*, *luck*, or *happenstance* are inadequate and inaccurate. Something more is happening than can be fully explained, something far greater than good fortune. In the thesaurus, there's a descriptive term under *providence* that doesn't appear under *coincidence*—"divine intervention." That sums up the difference between the two concepts. *Providence* is a word for believers.

This was best explained during our wedding when the pastor described how John and I met through God's providence. He said that many in the world might see our meeting in Ireland as coincidence. However, *coincidence* is a word for unbelievers, for it was indeed *providence*, the hand of God, that brought us together.[45] From that day forth, those words shaped how John and I view God's interaction in our lives.

We no longer deliberated the question, "Providence or coincidence, which one will it be?" The answer was apparent: providence.

Divine intervention is God's continual involvement in every moment of every day. He orchestrates the details of our lives so they fall in line with His plans and His purposes. For every providential way we see God working, there are countless behind-the-scenes moments that we miss. A kind word spoken at the right moment; the timeliness of stepping onto the elevator with a person we need to forgive; the car's warning light causing us to drive slower, thus preventing us from an accident; that check in our spirit that says, *Don't go there*. These occurrences all have the providential workings of something God-sent.

We need to wake up, be aware, and anticipate the unexpected ways that God is working. That means we have to slow down lest we miss something miraculous. We must ask Him to open our eyes, then wait expectantly for God to reveal Himself. In the words of C.S. Lewis,

> We may ignore, but we can nowhere evade, the presence of God. The world is crowded with [H]im. He walks everywhere incognito. And the incognito is not always hard to penetrate. The real labor is to remember, to attend, in fact to come awake, yet still more, to remain awake.[46]

Shared Blessings
In this book, I've acquainted you with my story and the marvelous ways that God has made me aware of His creative work in my life. I hope my words will point you to God, grow in you a deep desire for Jesus and the Holy Spirit's work in your life, and encourage you to reflect on your own story to discover how God is blessing you every day in the small things and on the grand scale. However, there's something more you should know: blessings are not something to keep for yourself. If you revel in the abundance of your blessings, hoard them for your pleasure alone, and allow no one else to know of them,

then you have completely missed the mark. Blessings are to be shared.

God told Abram, "And I will make you a great nation, and I will bless you, and make your name great; and so you shall be a blessing."[47]

You were blessed that you would be a blessing. Will you keep the blessings to yourself or will you share those blessings with others? Which one will it be?

How can we be a blessing to those around us? By living like the blessed people we are. Others observe our actions and our words; they notice when we display gratitude, peace, or contentment, even when the circumstances around us are unfavorable. On the flip side, people also recognize when we complain, argue, and grumble.

H. Norman Wright elaborates on this.

> No matter what happens during your day, you must remind yourself that you have been chosen for blessing, even if you just had an accident, lost your job, discovered you have cancer, or suffered a death in the family. These may be strong examples, but they represent the real world. No matter what happens, you are always a blessed person. You must learn to think and respond as a blessed person to all people and circumstances in your life.

He then cites the apostle Paul in Ephesians 4:1 (TLB), "I beg you . . . to live and act in a way worthy of those who have been chosen for such wonderful blessings as these."[48]

We also bless others by showing an interest in the people around us at home, in church, around the neighborhood, or inside our work environment. We tell them our story, the story of how God works in our lives and blesses us, and we point them to Jesus Christ.

Dan B. Allender wrote an entire book on knowing your

own personal story. He writes,

> Since we are called to tell our story, we are also called to listen to the stories of others. And since we are to tell and to listen, then even more so we are called to encourage others to know and tell and listen to God's story as well as their own. God is calling us to fully explore, to fully enjoy, and to fully capture the power of the Great Story, the gospel [of Jesus Christ]. And we are to invite others to immerse themselves in the Great Story. One way we do this is by listening to our lesser stories and then telling them to others.[49]

Scripture repeatedly says to tell of His glory and His wonderful acts, to speak of all His wonders, to make known His deeds.[50] Isaiah 12:5 even says, "Praise the Lord in song, for He has done excellent things; Let this be known throughout the earth." We read and hear these commands. However, excuses are made, apprehension escalates, and fear takes over. When this happens, we must ask the Holy Spirit for courage and boldness. He's in the business of achieving the unachievable and reaching the unreachable.

This book is meant to share the blessings that God has given me, because I don't want to keep them to myself. I encourage you to develop the habit of looking for God every day and enjoying the adventure of seeing Him in all the details of your life. In seeking God, listening for His voice, obeying, and trusting Him, you will discover God's involvement in your life in ways of which you never dreamed. As He responds, you may not have the same experiences as me, but you can be sure that when He says He'll respond, He will. God is the keeper of promises. He is also the source of all good things—showers upon showers of blessings (Ezekiel 34:26).

As you savor this heavenly flood, you may find yourself

saying to someone, "Would you like to hear my story? Let me tell you about my God. He is truly amazing. It's because of Him and what He has done that I live a blessed life!"

You are a channel of God's blessing.

Something to Consider
1. What are your thoughts on providence versus coincidence? How have you seen God working providentially in your life?
2. "Living like the blessed people that we are"—what does that look like in the life of a believer?
3. How can you be a blessing to other people? Who do you know that needs encouraging this week?

Further Reflection
- Genesis 12:2
- Ezekiel 34:26
- Romans 1:15–16
- Ephesians 4:1–3

ACKNOWLEDGMENTS

The room where I teach music has a great wall of windows smudged with small fingerprints from the children peering out. A car passing by, a cloud, a smile, a yellow butterfly, and a sunbeam all fit in this window. Like these little ones, press your nose to the glass and take a peek. This window offers you a view of the people who came along beside me on this book-writing adventure. They were essential in bringing this book to life. I humbly thank each one.

To my team of readers who faithfully read every word that I wrote, asked hard questions, encouraged me to keep at it, and offered advice and wisdom—John Coats, Max and Yvonne Kee, Lynn Coats, Jennifer Griffin, Rick and Claudia Davis, Tim and Wendy Koontz, Lisa McDonald, Mary Shelor. I am so thankful for each one of you.

To my prayer team who covered me in prayer through this whole process—John Coats, Max and Yvonne Kee, Greg and Jennifer Tinker, Brad and Lisa Oliver, Aaron and Stephanie Beazley, Bob and Lynn Coats, Mason and Jennifer Griffin, Rick and Claudia Davis, Tim and Wendy Koontz, Mary Shelor, Damian and Lisa McDonald, Theresa Seward, Barb Ostrowski, Mary Jane Davis, Rod and Christy Bakker, Lynn and Holly Gallagher, Becky Menke, Robin Delaney, Theresa Jones, Mitchel and Lacy Laman, Regina Wilhelm, Valerie Massey, and Lisa Patty. Most of you were with me from the start of this process, while others joined me on the way. Words cannot express how much I appreciate all of your prayers on my behalf.

To the countless others who are so dear to me and asked continually how things were going on the book and how they might pray for me. You know who you are!

To Rod Bakker, pastor and friend, I am grateful for your words to me personally and printed in this book. Thank you for your friendship and encouragement.

To Jennifer Tinker, Lisa Oliver, Robin Delaney, Claire Dagenhart, Lynda Harrington, and Jessica Brantley for reading my manuscript in whole. Your encouragement lifted my spirits and put a skip in my step.

To Raschelle Loudenslager, who spent hours with me on the phone talking about this book and the publishing process. Thank you for reading through my manuscript, commenting, and offering your expertise. I love it that you, cousin, are part of my story.

To my friend, Daniel Brantley—Your generous offer to help turn my manuscript into a book was a direct answer to prayer. I am deeply grateful for your editing, as well as your understanding and skill in the publishing process. I am proud to have Sir Brody on my book.

To Jennifer Griffin—I love your creativity. You captured what I was looking for beautifully in the cover design. Brava!

To Kris Berger—You have a way with the camera, my friend! Thank you for your patience with me.

To my breakfast ladies—Robin, Theresa, and Kim. There is nothing like sitting with kindred spirits, where you can simply be yourself in every way possible. You've supported me through the gamut of emotions I've gone through in writing this book. Thank you, friends.

To Trinity Presbyterian Church (PCA)—I'm especially grateful to the people at my church who help me grow toward maturity in Christ. Their prayers and love support me in so many ways.

To Fr. Ken Capalbo (aka Padre)—Thank you, friend, for your encouragement, prayers, listening ear, and friendship. Meeting you enriched the lives of the whole Coats family.

To my parents, Max and Yvonne Kee—Thank you for being such loving parents and introducing me to Jesus. You helped make me who I am today. Words cannot express my love for you both.

To all of my extended family and in-laws—Thank you for loving Jesus and following Him. What a privilege to call you my brothers and sisters in Christ.

To our children, David and Rachel—I appreciate your patience as I spent hours at my desk. You've been nothing but encouraging to me, cheering me on to finish this book. I'm so glad that God chose you two to be mine. I love you both the big ol' best!

To my husband, John Coats—My heart is full as I think of how to thank you, dearest husband. You've prayed for me and read my chapters two or three times before anyone else ever saw a word. Because of you, I've become a better writer than when this process began. You've captured my heart, John Daniel. Loving you has made me a blessed woman indeed!

To my Lord and Savior, Jesus Christ—I adore You! I long for the day when I'll finally see You face to face. Somehow, I know that Your arms will be open wide for me as I run into them. You're my best friend, and there are not enough words to express my love for You.

Thank you Father, for saying to me, *You are mine!*

This book is for You. May You alone receive all the glory and honor.

APPENDIX A

RECIPE FOR EASTER STORY COOKIES

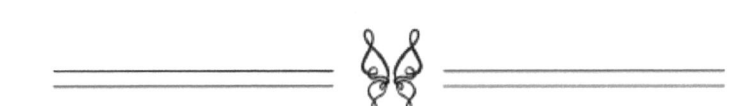

These cookies can be made at any time, but they are best when made the evening before Easter.

Ingredients
1 cup whole pecans
1 teaspoon vinegar
3 egg whites
Pinch of salt
1 cup sugar
1 wooden spoon
1 Ziploc® bag
Tape
A Bible

Instructions
1. Preheat oven to 300° F.
2. Place pecans in the Ziploc bag and let the children beat them with the wooden spoon to break them into small pieces. Explain that after Jesus was arrested, He was beaten by the Roman soldiers (John 19:1–3).

3. Let each child smell the vinegar. Put 1 teaspoon into a mixing bowl. Explain that when Jesus was thirsty on the cross, He was given vinegar to drink (John 19:28–30).

4. Add egg whites to the vinegar. Eggs represent life. Explain that Jesus gave His life to give us eternal life (John 10:10–11).

5. Sprinkle a little salt into each child's hand. Let each taste it and brush the rest into the bowl. Explain that this represents the salty tears shed by Jesus's followers and the bitterness of our own sin (Luke 23:27).

6. Add 1 cup sugar. Explain that the sweetest part of the story is that Jesus died because He loves us. He wants us to know and belong to Him (Psalm 34:8, John 3:16).

7. Beat with a mixer on high speed for 12–15 minutes, or until stiff peaks are formed. Explain that white represents the purity in God's eyes of those whose sins have been cleansed by Jesus (Isaiah 1:18, John 3:1–3).

8. Fold in the broken nuts. Drop the mix by teaspoons onto a wax paper-covered cookie sheet. Explain that each mound represents the rocky tomb where Jesus's body was laid (Matthew 27:57–60).

9. Put the cookie sheet in the oven, close the door, and turn the oven off. Give each child a piece of tape and seal the oven door. Explain that Jesus's tomb was sealed (Matthew 27:65–66).

10. Go to bed! Explain to the children that they may feel sad to leave the cookies in the oven overnight. Jesus's followers were in despair when the tomb was sealed (John 16:20, 22).

11. On Easter morning, open the oven and give everyone a cookie! Notice the cracked surface and take a bite. The cookies are hollow! On the first Easter, Jesus's followers were amazed to find the tomb open and empty (Matthew 28:1–9).

12. Enjoy Easter as you celebrate the resurrection of Jesus Christ.

APPENDIX B
WE BELONG TO GOD—WE ARE NOT OUR OWN

Old Testament Verses
Psalm 4:3
But know that the Lord has set apart the godly for Himself;
The Lord hears when I call to Him.

Psalm 24:1
The earth is the Lord's, and all it contains,
The world, and those who dwell in it.

Isaiah 43:1
But now, thus says the Lord, your Creator, O Jacob,
And He who formed you, O Israel,
"Do not fear, for I have redeemed you;
I have called you by name; you are Mine!"

Isaiah 43:7
"Everyone who is called by My name,
And whom I have created for My glory,
Whom I have formed, even whom I have made."

Ezekiel 18:4
"Behold, all souls are Mine; the soul of the father as well as the soul of the son is Mine. The soul who sins will die."

The verses from the Old Testament refer to Israel, God's chosen people. Those verses also speak to all followers of Jesus Christ, since we are chosen too. Paul explains in Ephesians 3:6 this very thing—that we, as Gentiles, are joined with Israel. It reads, "This mystery is that through the gospel the Gentiles are heirs together with Israel, members together of one body, and sharers together in the promise in Christ Jesus" (NIV).

New Testament Verses
John 10:14–15
Jesus says, "I am the good shepherd, and I know My own and My own know Me, even as the Father knows Me and I know the Father; and I lay down My life for the sheep."

John 17:1–2
Jesus spoke these things; and lifting up His eyes to heaven, He said, "Father, the hour has come; glorify Your Son, that the Son may glorify You, even as You gave Him authority over all flesh, that to all whom You have given Him, He may give eternal life."

John 17:9–10
[Jesus speaking:] "I ask on their behalf; I do not ask on behalf of the world, but of those whom You have given Me; for they are Yours; and all things that are Mine are Yours, and Yours are Mine; and I have been glorified in them."

Acts 17:24–28
The God who made the world and all things in it, since He is Lord of heaven and earth, does not dwell in temples made with hands; nor is He served by human hands, as though He needed

anything, since He Himself gives to all people life and breath and all things; and He made from one man every nation of mankind to live on all the face of the earth, having determined their appointed times and the boundaries of their habitation, that they would seek God, if perhaps they might grope for Him and find Him, though He is not far from each one of us; for in Him we live and move and exist, as even some of your own poets have said, "For we also are His children."

Romans 14:7–8
For not one of us lives for himself, and not one dies for himself; for if we live, we live for the Lord, or if we die, we die for the Lord; therefore whether we live or die, we are the Lord's.

1 Corinthians 6:13
Food is for the stomach and stomach is for food, but God will do away with both of them. Yet the body is not for immorality, but for the Lord, and the Lord is for the body.

1 Corinthians 6:17
But the one who joins himself to the Lord is one spirit with Him.

1 Corinthians 6:19–20
Or do you not know that your body is a temple of the Holy Spirit who is in you, whom you have from God, and that you are not your own? For you have been bought with a price: therefore glorify God in your body.

1 Corinthians 8:6
Yet for us there is but one God, the Father, from whom are all things, and we exist for Him; and one Lord, Jesus Christ, by whom are all things, and we exist through Him.

Ephesians 1:3-4
Blessed be the God and Father of our Lord Jesus Christ, who has blessed us with every spiritual blessing in the heavenly places in Christ, just as He chose us in Him before the foundation of the world, that we would be holy and blameless before Him.

Ephesians 1:13-14
In Him, you also, after listening to the message of truth, the gospel of your salvation—having also believed, you were sealed in Him with the Holy Spirit of promise, who is given as a pledge of our inheritance, with a view to the redemption of God's own possession, to the praise of His glory.

NOTES

1. Taken from The Holy Bible, New International Version, ©1973, 1978 by the International Bible Society, used by permission of Zondervan Bible Publishers.
This book opens with the quote from the New International Version (NIV), because that was the version I was reading when the verse came to my attention and God used it in my life. Unless otherwise noted, all other Scripture quotations are from the New American Standard translation.
2. Herbert Lockyer Sr., *Nelson's Illustrated Bible Dictionary* (Nashville, TN: Thomas Nelson, 1986), 185.
3. Jim Weidmann, "Building a Heritage," Crosswalk.com, 21, Sept. 2002, http://www.crosswalk.com/family/parenting/building-a-heritage-1149364.html (accessed 6 April 2012).
4. Charles Stanley, *How To Keep Your Kids on Your Team* (Nashville, TN: Thomas Nelson Publishers, 1986), 102.
5. Billy Graham, *Angels: God's Secret Agents* (Dallas, TX: Word Publishing, 1986), 24.
6. Graham, *Angels*, 10, 32.
7. Graham, *Angels*, 76.
8. Andrew Murray, *The Andrew Murray Daily Reader in To-*

day's Language (Minneapolis, MN: Bethany House, 2005), 118.

9. Rick Warren, *The Purpose Driven Life* (Grand Rapids, MI: Zondervan, 2002), 273.

10. If you have never heard Dr. Lockridge's sermon, "That's My King," I highly recommend you look him up on the internet (see S. M. Lockridge, "That's My King," 1979, https://vimeo.com/66414021, accessed 11 June 2019). Pull up the sermon, close your eyes, and really listen. It is very powerful.

11. J.I. Packer, *Knowing God* (Downers Grove, IL: InterVarsity Press, 1973), 123.

12. Packer, *Knowing God*, 126.

13. Max Anders, *New Christian's Handbook: Everything New Believers Need to Know* (Nashville, TN: Thomas Nelson, Inc, 1999), 143.

14. I have changed the names in this story to respect the privacy of these ladies.

15. Bill Bright, *The Joy of Supernatural Thinking: Believing God for the Impossible* (Colorado Springs, CO: Cook Communications Ministries, 2005), 31.

16. Philip Yancey, *Reaching for the Invisible God: What Can We Expect to Find?* (Grand Rapids, MI: Zondervan, 2000), 181.

17. "Big church" was what my family called the church worship services when I was a little girl.

18. Words by Judson W. Van DeVenter; "I Surrender All," 1896; http://www.cyberhymnal.org/htm/i/s/isurrend.htm (Accessed 3 Dec. 2008).

19. Kay Arthur, 31, Oct. 2003, http://dailychristianquote.com/dcqarthur.html (accessed 16 Jan. 2009).

20. Elisabeth Elliot, 21, May 2008, http://dailychristianquote.com/dcqelliot.html#eliz (accessed 21 Jan. 2009).

21. Max Anders, *30 Days to Understanding the Bible in 15 Minutes a Day!* (Nashville, TN: Thomas Nelson Publishers, 1998).

22. Richard J. Foster, *Prayer: Finding the Heart's True Home* (San Francisco, CA: Harper Collins Publishers, 1992), 227.

23. Henri J. M. Nouwen in Lenya Heitzig and Penny Pierce Rose's book, *Pathway to God's Plan: Ruth and Esther* (Wheaton, IL: Tyndale House Publishers, 2002), 159.
24. "Beauty for Ashes." Words and music by Crystal Lewis. ©1996 Metro One.
25. Cursillo and Walk to Emmaus are four-day spiritual retreats. Cursillo is sponsored by the Catholic diocese while Walk to Emmaus is rooted in the Methodist tradition.
26. The perspective of our friend Rick, who with the help of our other friend Tim, called everybody to this gathering of prayer on my behalf, to which I am forever grateful.
Scripture texts used in his quote are taken from the New American Bible, revised edition ©1986, Confraternity of Christian Doctrine (CCD), Washington, DC.
27. A comment made by the late Art Witte, one of our friends from the Cursillo community. Art, who was experiencing his own sufferings, mentioned this to John in hopes of encouraging us.
28. Yancey, *Reaching for the Invisible God*, 283.
29. Romans 8:28.
30. Foster, *Prayer*, 220.
31. "All Who Are Thirsty." Words and music by Brenton Brown and Glenn Robertson. ©1998 Vineyard Songs.
32. St. Augustine, www.quoteworld.org/quotes/9965 (accessed 20 Aug. 2008).
33. 1 Corinthians 12:8–10; See Ephesians 4:7–13 and Romans 12:3–8 for similar lists.
34. H. Norman Wright, *Chosen for Blessing* (Eugene, OR: Harvest House Publishing, 1992), 160.
35. "Dive." Words and music by Steven Curtis Chapman. ©1999 Speechless. Sparrow Records.
36. See Psalm 37:7, NIV.
37. H. Norman Wright, *Experiencing Grief* (Nashville, TN: B & H Publishing Group, 2004), 76.

38. If you are in the middle of a move, I encourage you to read the helpful advice from Susan Miller's book, *After the Boxes are Unpacked: Moving On After Moving In*. This book ministered to me during our move to Illinois, and then, ten years later to Tennessee. See also http//www.justmoved.org/.

39. Eugene Peterson, *Working the Angles* (Grand Rapids, MI: Eerdmans, 1987), 30–31.

40. Philip Yancey, *Prayer: Does It Make Any Difference?* (Grand Rapids, MI: Zondervan, 2006), 32.

41. Ruth Haley Barton, *Invitation to Solitude and Silence: Experiencing God's Transforming Presence* (Downers Grove, IL: InterVarsity Press, 2004), 96.

42. Andrew Murray, *Humility: The Journey Toward Holiness* (Minneapolis, MN: Bethany House, 2001), 72–73.

43. J.I. Packer & Carolyn Nystrom, *Praying: Finding Our Way Through Duty to Delight* (Downers Grove, IL: InterVarsity Press, 2006), 125.

44. Isaiah 43:1. God spoke these words to Israel, His chosen people. Israel had entered a covenant with God, which was initiated first through Abraham. So if you belong to Christ, then you are Abraham's offspring, heirs according to promise (Galatians 3:29). These words are for you, who are new creations in Jesus Christ!

45. Dr. Gene Wilkes, president of B. H. Carroll Theological Institute, is both a pastor and an author, in addition to being my youth pastor growing up. He is very special to me, and I am appreciative of his words of blessing.

46. C.S. Lewis, *Letters to Malcolm: Chiefly on Prayer* (London: Geoffrey Bles, 1964), 100–101.

47. Genesis 12:2—I can hear it now, "But that is the Old Testament; it does not apply to us." It does! I have addressed this in the previous chapter in an endnote as well as in Appendix B.

48. Wright, *Chosen for Blessing*, 171. Wright is using The Living Bible.

49. Dan B. Allender, *To Be Told: Know Your Stories, Shape Your Future* (Colorado Springs, CO: WaterBrook Press, 2005), 4.
50. 1 Chronicles 16:8–9, 24; also, the Psalms are full of these references.

www.ingramcontent.com/pod-product-compliance
Lightning Source LLC
Chambersburg PA
CBHW030326100526
44592CB00010B/585